To Dee, with many
thanks again for all
your help –
Sincerely,
Lucy

Y0-ABG-337

LUCY'S TWENTIETH CENTURY

Portrait painted by Felix DeCossio in New York City in 1970

Family group, taken in Berkeley, California, 6/27/71 by Bob Lynds, photographer.

Left to right:

Back row standing:

Norman McIntyre, Ovid H. Ritter, Jr., Michael Ritter, Jean Claude Heraud, Irving Ritter.

Middle row seated:

Mrs. N.R. McIntyre (nee Lucianne Ritter) with daughter, Talley McIntyre on lap, Mrs. Ovid H. Ritter, Lucy E. Ritter, Mrs. Michael Ritter with son John Ritter on lap, Mrs. Jean Claude Heraud (nee Nancy Ritter), Mrs. Irving Ritter.

Middle row standing:

Patricia Ritter, daughter of Mr. and Mrs. Michael Ritter.

Front row seated:

Trevor McIntyre, Todd McIntyre, Marc Heraud, Alain Heraud.

LUCY ELIZABETH RITTER

LUCY'S TWENTIETH CENTURY

Illustrated with half-tones and 4-color photographs

VANTAGE PRESS

New York   Washington   Hollywood

FIRST EDITION

All rights reserved, including the right of reproduction in whole or in part in any form.

Copyright © 1974 by Lucy Elizabeth Ritter

Published by Vantage Press, Inc. 516 West 34th Street, New York, New York 10001

Manufactured in the United States of America

Standard Book No. 533-00964-2

DEDICATED WITH ADMIRATION AND LOVE
TO MY BROTHERS AND SISTER
OVID HERBERT RITTER, JR.
IRVING OSBORN RITTER
MARGARET RITTER FRANTZ

ACKNOWLEDGMENTS

The pictures depicting Chinese scenes were done by my godfather, Mr. J. Orram Sheppard. He was a businessman whose hobby was photography, and he was a real artist. As mentioned in the text, he died a prisoner of war of the Japanese in Stanley Prison in Hong Kong during World War II. Since he left no immediate family to call attention to his work, it is my privilege to use it here, hoping that my readers will appreciate his great talent.

I also wish to thank Mr. DeWitt Bishop of Sacramento for his help and patience in preparing the photography so it could be used in this work.

My cousin, Mr. Norman Ritter, Vice President of Squibb Corporation in New York City, was most helpful to me in bringing this work to fruition, and I wish to express my gratitude to him.

CONTENTS

LUCY'S TWENTIETH CENTURY

PROLOGUE

THE TURBULENT 20th Century is now into its waning years, and what history it encompasses! Having been born in the early years of this kaleidoscopic, imaginative, tempestuous era, my life has touched many of the facets of its course, and it is in my heart to record some of these episodes.

My early childhood in a British Crown Colony tasted of the best of the British colonial life; my parents, both young Stanford graduates, embarked on a business career in the Orient and identified themselves with old China hands. I was treated to a fascinating trip to Peking, the Summer Palace, the Great Wall, private school in Hong Kong, and other treasures only now coming to view again for Western eyes.

My family returned to the States, and there were high school and Stanford University in the heyday of the post-World War I years, when a war had been fought to outlaw war and make the world safe for democracy. This was the era of the flapper and the Charleston. Came the Depression when my generation was tested to its roots and remained generally loyal, patriotic, industrious and dedicated to a constructive and compassionate life. They led the U.S. to an unsurpassed standard of living.

These Depression years were the patient years—more pay cuts than raises—reduced working schedules, haunting desires for fun and activity and never any money. And youth was vanishing. Those who lived through the Depression will carry its scars to their graves; they also carry a great strength and courage. That generation did not quit and did not destroy.

Then came World War II and the tremendous drive and mobilization to win the war—which we did. A great political awareness subsequently developed; everybody was in the act, and I had the never-to-be-forgotten experience of attending two Democratic National Conventions as a delegate—one which nominated Adlai Stevenson in the Stock Yards of

Chicago and the other, Lyndon Johnson on the boardwalk of Atlantic City. And what a contrast!—which I shall describe subsequently.

In the interim I had been women's Co-Chairman of Citizens for Kennedy in my area, ridden the Kennedy campaign train with that magnificent young leader, shared the exultation of victory and hope and the abysmal despair of the assassination. Our country lost something when the young Kennedys were murdered, and we haven't won it back yet.

I was earning my living during all these adult years and participated in the struggle for women to be allowed to apply for jobs for which they were capable. As my retirement looms closer my company has honored me with the title of Vice President—Securities and placed me in charge of a $200 million portfolio and Governor Pat Brown appointed me to the State Retirement Board which ran a $4½ billion fund. I served on this Board nine years.

This has been an era which loved beauty, when the U.S.A. seemed to come of age culturally, having leisure at long last for the development of the arts. There have been great symphony orchestras developed; a world of painting, sculpture, and art collecting; the growth of great universities. Broadway and off-Broadway have been fun, and business trips to New York City have made it possible to share the beauty of Gertrude Lawrence in *The King and I*, the spirit of Ethel Merman in *Call Me Madam*, the wistfulness of Gwen Verdon in *Red Head*, the spirit of America in *Damn Yankees* and the wit of the French in *La Plume de Ma Tante* and *Coco* and the nostalgia of my own age in *No, No, Nanette* with Ruby Keeler.

There have been great trips abroad from the North Cape to Buenos Aires and Capetown and repeated visits to magnificent London and Paris.

It has been a scintillating age in which a little working girl could share in the pot of gold at the end of the rainbow. May I share my reminiscences with you—in the spirit that we have much to cherish and love, and use as an inspiration to build even higher, turning our backs upon despair and defeat? At the same time hopefully, common sense can guide our steps.

So, let us begin.

FAMILY BACKGROUND

MY PARENTS were born in the late 19th Century. My father was a red-blooded American liberal, whose family went back to the first Michael Ritter who arrived in Pennsylvania with the Pennsylvania Dutch, and subsequently walked all the way to New York's Finger Lake Region and built a sturdy stone house on Lake Cayuga, a house which was to remain in the family for 100 years. My father's mother, born in Denmark, lived for many years in the old stone farmhouse and bathed her sons and did her laundry in water she pumped from the well behind the house. And somehow she found time to do oil paintings of the surrounding landscape.

My mother was a blue-blooded aristocrat, who traced her line on one side to American revolutionaries who participated in the Revolution, and on the other side she was a Jennings, straight down from the line of the redoubtable, redheaded Sarah Jennings who became Sarah Churchill, the first Duchess of Marlborough and a forebear of the great Winston Churchill. These same Jenningses had a *papier-maché* factory and hobnobbed with Josiah Wedgewood over their respective crafts. Another strain in the family was the Corker family—of old Northumbrian vintage—who subsequently moved to Ireland and were known as the Corkers from Cork. As Protestants in Ireland this family had its tempestuous moments, as did my own gentle mother, who later grew up in Salt Lake City, granddaughter of a Presbyterian and an Episcopalian minister, both of whom battled the Mormons.

I mention these different strains in my parents' ancestry because it was remarkable how alike they were in their respect for human dignity, their compassion for their fellow beings, their reverence for learning and also their self-discipline. They taught us never to mar or deface a book—they were raised in a period when books were hard to come by. We were reared to believe that the only true aristocracy in the world was the aristocracy of the intellect.

As young people they both attended and graduated from Stanford University, a privately endowed school destined to become the Harvard of the West. They both worked for their education, for by the time they came along their own immediate forebears had become too cultured to care very much about making money. Fighting the U.S. Revolution, crossing the country to Illinois, Utah, Nevada and then California left little energy for amassing wealth. My parents were both put to it to provide for themselves, and this they did.

My mother grew up in Salt Lake City and all her life retained her love for the mountains which were her natural habitat. Her father was interested in gold mining, and was sometimes in funds and sometimes out of them. This environment led her to view with considerable trepidation my first stock market investments, as she had lived with financial uncertainty. Her mother moved to Palo Alto and took in boarders while my mother went to Stanford. She was tall and had burnished golden red hair and blue eyes, and pictures show her as Queen Elizabeth in an early Stanford dramatic production. She loved Stanford at the turn of the century, and made the acquaintance of the great old David Starr Jordan, the first president of the University, a real scholar and a truly wise man.

How thrilled I was many years later likewise to make the acquaintance of this white-maned old sage with the cane and have him tell me he remembered my parents.

My mother also became very fond of Mrs. Branner, whose husband was the next president of Stanford.

My father was a medical patient of Dr. Ray Lyman Wilbur, who also was a president of Stanford. My father indeed was Ray Lyman Wilbur's first smallpox patient and recounted the episode of ringing Wilbur's doorbell to find out what ailed him and of Wilbur's sternly ordering him not to come a step closer. He was immediately put in an isolation ward and brought back to health by the stern and brilliant, and inviolate Wilbur.

14

Great men and great students participated to build Stanford; and when destructive students today bomb the classrooms, knock the books off the library shelves and damage the campus bookstore, they get no sympathy from me. How little the arrogant activists appreciate the dedicated efforts of an earlier generation to build a seat of learning.

When I heard a former Stanford student body president speak at the investiture of a new university president and make the claim that his generation had all the solid virtues, I wondered how he could so lightly dismiss the subject of their lack of self-discipline.

But back to my family. My father came from a line of educated farmers. His father, having left the family farm on Lake Cayuga, New York, emigrated across the country, did a stint as a surveyor in Nevada and graduated from Stanford as an older man, winning a Phi Beta Kappa key in the process. Grandpa was for many years principal of Stockton High School, and a stern disciplinarian he was. Many an elderly lady in Stockton told me that Grandpa had rapped her knuckles with a ruler while she was a student in his class. Grandpa's principal problem then appeared to be my handsome Uncle Irving, who covered the ceilings of his classrooms with his spit balls, and subsequently became a Westinghouse engineer. Grandpa was later principal of Chico Normal School—a predecessor of Chico State College. My father took us all up to Chico to visit after we had returned from the Orient and was proud to show off the tree lined streets, Bidwell Park and other points of interest of his early Chico days.

My grandfather was a charming man. I remember some beautiful letters he wrote me on such occasions as my fifth and sixth birthdays. And I also remember the economies he practiced. When we visited him as children we had to study in the same room in which he was sitting, because we were not allowed to have the electric lights on in any more rooms than strictly necessary.

Grandpa was a mathematician and a classical scholar. In fact, he published a mathematics text book. He required my father to major in Latin at Stanford.

15

My practical father was so disgusted with the uselessness of this major that he eliminated Latin entirely from my studies, which was really considered a heresy at that time.

My father was raised to be a scholar and went to Stanford University and was active on the debating team. He trained to be a teacher, as did my mother; and both of them taught for a couple of years upon graduation in such spots as Mendocino, Lakeport and Fowler. My father's practical nature was soon to take the ascendancy over the professorial and he decided to go into business. He secured a position with the old Pacific Mail Steamship Company and went to Shanghai as passenger agent. When he left for Shanghai he had already become engaged to my mother, and after six months in Shanghai he decided he was able to support his bride-to-be and he sent for her to come. She arrived in Shanghai and they were married by the late John Nichols, who was subsequently to become Bishop of the Shanghai territory. My parents went for a never-to-be forgotten honeymoon on a houseboat on the Yangtze-Kiang River. As children we were treated to many stories and pictures of this excursion. My mother told me that Daddy assured her that she did not need to be nervous of the Chinese, and I'm sure she never was. She became very fond of the Chinese in her 14 years of life in China.

They settled in Shanghai and my father was rapidly advanced. By the time he left the Orient after 14 years he was manager for the company of all the Pacific offices—Hong Kong, Shanghai, Manila, Yokohama and Kobe and had lived variously in both Hong Kong and Shanghai. In those days the U.S. had a concession of extraterritorial rights in Shanghai, so when we children were born our births were registered with the American consul, which had the technical affect of our births being treated just as if we had been born on United States soil.

Shanghai was a glamorous city in those days. It was one of the great ports of the world, with people of every nationality making it their home.

My parents' friends included American oil people, chemists, German doctors, English business men, white Russians and a number of Episcopalians who ran St. John's College in

Shanghai. My father joined the American volunteers, and we children were fascinated by pictures of Daddy in his soldier's uniform carrying a gun. My mother joined the women's basketball team, and the pictures of these beautiful Gibson girls with ankle length skirts playing basketball were something to remember. We had wonderful Sunday picnics in the tenders on the River and excursions into the countryside.

One of my earliest recollections is of the American Consul dressing up as Santa Claus and bringing Christmas presents to my brother Ovid and me. But even then I knew he was the Consul. My most memorable recollection of this Shanghai period was the overnight train trip to Peking when we stayed at the old *Wagon-Lits* Hotel. We took walks on the Peking Wall and had tea on the marble boat at the Summer Palace. The Summer Palace was built with a million dollars which the Dowager Queen had raised to build a Chinese Navy, but the Summer Palace appealed to her more after she had the money. We have spectacular pictures of this trip—of the Temple of Heaven and the Altar of Heaven and the beautiful walkways at the Summer Palace.

I was fascinated recently at the pictures in *Life Magazine* which showed our tennis team at the Marble Boat. To think it is still there! How many years it has been since people traveled freely to Peking, and how fortunate to have this wonderful memory!

Life was rigorous as well as fascinating. All drinking water had to be boiled and we never ate fresh fruits or vegetables unless they had been washed in permanganate of potash. Great was the dread of cholera and with reason. Of the young couples who were friends of my family, we were the only ones who did not lose a child. I well remember my mother saying upon our departure, "Old Bubbling Well Cemetery never got one of my children."

Without her constant care of her family, we never would have survived.

HONG KONG

I HAVE more recollections of Hong Kong, as it is there I went to school.

We lived in a beautiful house on the Peak overlooking Hong Kong Harbor. Our house had high ceilings and wide verandas, upstairs and downstairs, and at the front, back, and side. We lived constantly with the beautiful view of Hong Kong Harbor before us, and it instilled in me a love of the ocean and water which has always been a part of me. In fact I learned to walk on a ship sailing the high seas—on the old *Korea* which was one of the ships in my father's company. Hong Kong Harbor is not really a large harbor, as harbors go, and we could see the ships of the world as they steamed into port. We could identify them; the old Empress ships, the PEO, Blue Funnel, Mathison Jardine, and our own *China*. The *China* was with my father's line and she used to be called the Queen of the Pacific because she was so graceful.

We went to school at the Peak School—a private school maintained primarily for children of British diplomats and business people. There were only 50 Americans in Hong Kong at that time and we Ritters were six of them. We were welcomed into the school and the instruction was practically on an individual basis. It was a beautiful school at the top of the Peak. It was bombed during the War and is no longer standing.

We rode the cable car up the Peak to school every day. The tramway still has the same names for the cars—the *Green Eye* and the *White Eye*—or did the last time I was in Hong Kong. It was too far to go home for lunch, or tiffin as it was invariably called then. Therefore our coolie brought us a hot lunch from home every day, carefully packed in a rattan basket with heating units.

We played with English and Scottish children and developed a lifelong fondness for them.

Among our good friends was the Stabb family. Their father was the head of the Hong Kong Shanghai Banking Corporation and they lived in a big house on the top of the hill. He was knighted when they returned to England years later. The boy my age in the family became an RAF pilot and was shot down by the Germans during the War. The girl my age was married to a boy who was also a casualty in the War. But the family held its head high in spite of tragedy. What a price those great English families paid to protect their country! England always sent the flower of her youth off to war. It was *noblesse oblige*.

One of my most charming recollections was of our Sunday swimming parties. We would take a launch out to Repulse Bay—picnic and all. I remember that my dear Godfather (a New Zealander who was my father's closest friend) would put me in a lifebuoy and swim with me to the beach. What a thrill for a six-year-old to be allowed to swim all the way in from the launch! What happy days those were!

Later, when the war came, this same dear godfather, by then a man in his fifties, was taken prisoner by the Japanese, and marched, along with the other whites, from Repulse Bay into the center of town and thrown into Stanley Prison. The prisoners were fed fish and water there; he contracted dysentery, was denied medical attention, and died. Ah, man's inhumanity to man!

We used to take trips to Manila sometimes. This was fun too. We would stay at the old Manila Hotel. My family had good friends, Carlos Young from Utah and the Baldwins—all with Macondray and Co. We would play with the Baldwin children, and they used to visit us many years later in Stockton. When the war came they were all thrown into Santa Tomas Prison, and only the strong ones survived. Those who did live attributed their good fortune to the loyalty and perseverance of their old Filipino servants who smuggled food into them through the barbed wire fence at night, at risk to their own lives. Their business was wiped out during the war, but they built it back after the holocaust was over.

My father and mother entertained a great deal. I remember the lovely dinner parties, the formal service at our large teakwood dining set (which I subsequently gave to the

Stanford Home for Girls in Sacramento). Occasionally my mother would allow my older brother Ovid and me to sit down with the guests; they were from all over the world.

We lived across the street from a private hotel called Kingsclair, which had originally been built as a private mansion by Parsees from India. I still remember the polished shining floors in the ball room, where even the Prince of Wales (the later Duke of Windsor) made official appearances for his country.

Life was at a much more leisured pace in those faraway days. When I later returned to Hong Kong, the private homes including our own beautiful one, had iron grills across the windows and verandas. Life had become much more dangerous after the Communists drove thousands of refugees from the mainland into Hong Kong. Many of the refugees became beggars as it was impossible for so many to find work in Hong Kong and they didn't have valid passports to be accepted anywhere else.

I remember being entertained at the Governor's mansion. They had children's parties some times. I remember frequent walks through the beautiful Cathedral grounds. I received my early training as an Episcopalian in this branch of the Church of England. Then there were the beautiful botanical gardens where we often played. And there was an old stone house nearby called the Stonecutters' house. Whenever there was a funeral the Chinese who lived there would start their wailing ritual. The soft summer evenings are still associated in my mind with the singsong music from the Stonecutters' house.

We took trips to Canton and visited with friends at the Canton Christian College. Daddy's Chinese friends in Canton entertained us sumptuously and I remember the dinners of many courses at which we children were fortunately included. I remember we really had bird's nest soup and sharkfin soup. I remember also the zoo at the top of the big store in Canton (I think the name was Sun's) and the huge snakes lying coiled in their cages and tortoises which seemed absolutely gigantic to my young eyes. Then there were visits to the mission schools and we watched the little children making beautiful lace—a hard life for those little children, but the alternative was abandonment if the missions did not care for them. There was a trip also to Macao and its fantan dens. This famous game consisted of no more than counting out Chinese coins in units of four and betting how many coins would be left over. There were frequent rides in rickshaws and sedan chairs, and I know now that few of the Chinese coolies who operated these vehicles lived beyond their thirties. Tuberculosis caught up with them.

I had two brothers and a little sister. My brothers were named Ovid, who has been in shipping all his life; Irving, now business manager of San Quentin Prison, and my married sister, Mrs. Arthur Frantz who lives in New York city and has pursued a professional singing career. We had many happy hours together and share many pleasant memories.

Our household was full of servants, this being the pattern of those days. The staff usually consisted of a No. 1 houseboy, a No. 2 houseboy, a coolie, cook, amah, and extra hands in the cook house. We did not have automatic plumbing, so a commode man came every day to empty the toilets. The bathroom floors were slanting, so when we pulled the corks out of the bathtubs the water ran down the slanting floors to drains which took it out.

We had beautiful furniture, a beautiful home, an idyllic life. Why did it come to an end? When the time came for my older brother and me to go on to higher than elementary school my parents had to choose between breaking up the family and sending us home, or severing their own ties. They chose not to follow the English system of sending the children away but decided to move the whole family. It was a decision which I know tore them to their souls. They were both successful and attractive. But they were too warm-hearted to break up their family. So they moved to the States in their middle years to start over. It was a hard decision for they never again had the money they had in the Orient. But they had their family intact.

I have recited the calamities that befell our English friends, our Manila friends and my godfather—who stayed on until war came. My family did not lose their loved ones; they only lost their financial advantages. And as the tragedies of the war unfolded and deepened, time proved that their decision was correct. They preserved their family and became associ-

21

ated with a university which they were instrumental in saving.

They made their decision while World War I was deepening. I remember as a little girl going to the Red Cross Headquarters in Hong Kong with my mother and ripping yards of selvage and rolling it into balls and cutting scraps to stuff pillows.

Daddy sent his family home first. We stopped at the old Stewart Hotel in San Francisco. Then my mother took her little flock to the high Sierras to visit her brother who was a surveyor for the Michigan-California Lumber Co. We visited in a lumber camp named Pino Grande near Georgetown and went to school in Georgetown for a few months. A greater contrast could not be imagined; private school in Hong Kong to public school in Georgetown in California's mother lode country. The country was magnificent. There were great trips up and down the American River Canyon, up to Loon Lake and Wentworth Springs where we hiked over huge granite boulders. It was a taste of American mountains at their greatest.

When Daddy closed up his business and came home, we went to New York and visited in New York City, Geneva in upstate New York, sampled the snow of a New York winter, and eventually settled in Stockton, California.

And thereby opens a new chapter.

Chinese ladies and old auto, taken about 1910.

Shanghai Volunteers, taken about 1907.

Ritter family residence in Hong Kong. No. 3, McDonald Road—on the Peak.

Street Scene in Hong Kong, showing rickshaws and sedan chairs in daily use, about 1917.

Altar of Heaven, showing Sacrificial Vats in foreground, Peking, China.

Photography by Mr. J. Orram Sheppard, Godfather to writer, taken about 1915.

Chinese Children in Hong Kong.

Photography by Mr. J. Orram Sheppard, Godfather to the writer, taken about 1915.

Chinese Water Buffalo.

Photography by Mr. J. Orram Sheppard, Godfather to the writer. Taken about 1915.

Temple of Heaven, Peking, China.

Photography by Mr. J. Orram Sheppard, Godfather to the writer, taken about 1915.

Chinese children in Hong Kong about 1917.

Photography by
Mr. J. Orram Sheppard,
Godfather to writer,
taken about 1915.

View of Summer Palace in Peking, China.

Photography by Mr. J. Orram Sheppard, Godfather to the writer, taken about 1915.

Chinese Women Weavers.

Photography by Mr. J. Orram Sheppard, Godfather to writer. Taken in Hong Kong about 1915.

Chinese Gentleman.

Photography by Mr. J. Orram Sheppard, Godfather to writer. Taken in Hong Kong about 1915.

Walkway at Summer Palace in Peking, China.

Photography by Mr. J. Orram Sheppard, Godfather to writer, taken about 1915.

Detail of walkway
at Summer Palace
in Peking, China.

Photography by
Mr. J. Orram Sheppard,
Godfather to writer,
taken about 1915.

STOCKTON

HIGH SCHOOL years spent in Stockton, a small city then of some 40,000, were a reflection of much that was typical of America. We lived in a Dutch Colonial house, with five bedrooms and a beautiful garden, and we lived comfortably by 1920 standards. There was no air conditioning, and the upstairs of our house was so hot on summer afternoons and evenings that no one went upstairs. At that time it would never have occurred to anyone to consider himself underprivileged because he was hot and spent some sleepless night in July and August when he couldn't cool off. There was no central heat upstairs, and we all dressed in winter months around a wood stove in the center hall upstairs. Nevertheless this was a very comfortable home. Our beautiful Chinese furniture lent it an air of distinction, and my father's green thumb provided us with a garden full of camellias, lush acacia trees, prize winning rose bushes and exquisite flowering fruit trees. We were in a subdivision named Tuxedo Park; we were on the edge of town and our beloved old chow dog could chase rabbits in the fields two blocks from our house.

I choose to describe our life in Stockton in some detail. In so doing perhaps I can recapture for a moment something precious of an era that has gone.

We attended Stockton High School, where my grandfather had been a former principal. We had truly dedicated teachers, and they gave their students a real education. Stockton prided itself on its excellent English Department and the fact that most of its graduates passed the "bonehead English" exams that all college freshmen were required to take. It was a big school for those days—a couple of thousand in attendance. It was well disciplined. It would never have occurred to anyone to participate in a riot or public march. It was completely safe to go to school on one's bicycle or on the street car. This was before the age of car pools or bussing and mothers did not have to take the time to get their children to school. We had contests of all sorts. The boys had their basketball, football and track teams and the town turned out to support them—the same as now. There were various scholastic competitions; we made the Honor Scholarship Society if our grades were good enough; we participated in debating and public speaking contests. I remember being chosen to represent my school in an extemporaneous speaking contest; my parents drove me to Turlock, a neighboring small town, and we drew our subjects and mine was "Wilson—The Misunderstood Hero." I won second place, and was very pleased.

Our parents participated in community activities. My father belonged to Rotary Club and was treasurer of the Haggin Art Gallery for many years. Our closest connection with the stock market crash came when it developed that the then president of the New York Stock Exchange (later imprisoned) used some of the Haggin Art Gallery securities in his speculations.

My mother was president of the Philomathean Club, the ladies' cultural effort, which brought many of the country's intellectuals to Stockton. I remember that Meiklejohn, president of Amherst, came to talk to us; as did Edgar Lee Masters of Spoon River Anthology, John Powys, Louis Untermeyer, and Emma Goldman, my first encounter with a Communist. My mother also belonged to the DAR, and their principal effort then was developing the blood bank, which was a great achievement.

These classes produced Douglas Fuller who is a leading Chicago banker and Melvin Belli, conspicuous for his considerable legal activity.

We had proper little parties to which we were properly chaperoned. The greatest issue which I can remember was whether or not high school sororities should be allowed. We were surely poor by today's standards, but no one knew it. The Charleston was coming in and we all learned it. We had short skirts, and then long skirts, and flapper hair do's. It was rumored that a girl at school had had an illegitimate baby, but one case did not create a social problem. We pursued our busy little lives.

I graduated from high school in 1926 and was fortunate in being admitted to Stanford. I adored Stanford. Having graduated from high school at 15 my first experiences of adulthood were at Stanford, and how exciting it was.

I am reminded that these were the days when *Babbitt* was written, belittling small-town America. It was materialistic—in retrospect—and we were building for the Depression, but a teenager never sensed these problems. Social lines were drawn which were too inflexible, it is true. But there was so much that was good then. Life had a simple quality. Families spent much more time together than they do now. Less adequate transportation kept people home more. Activities centered around the home more. If there were artificial social standards there was also more enjoyment of simple pleasures. Families worked together, shared together, loved their country, and children accepted their parents' discipline.

We rolled off to summer camping trips at Lake Tahoe in the family Oldsmobile, always accompanied by our chow dog Teddy. There were harrowing moments when the water boiled in the motor as we ascended the Sierras. A particularly traumatic memory is of the car rolling backwards down hill when the brakes failed to hold, and there was a train coming on the tracks below. But we got out of that one—as we did most emergencies. Everyone else had the same experiences, so it did not occur to anyone to feel that life was hard. Beautiful Tahoe was at the end of the road, and it took all day to get there. We usually started our camping expeditions at 3 o'clock in the morning to allow for the unexpected. If sometimes there were bats in the tent at Tahoe, there were also the beautiful whispering pines and redwoods above us, and the magnificent Lake before us. So we returned time and again.

STANFORD

STANFORD was a high point in my life. It had been a goal to me to attend my parents' alma mater. At that time the enrollment of women students was held to 500, and it took some doing to be included in that illustrious group. Luck was with me, and I made it. I spent five years there, receiving my A.B. degree when I was 19 and my master's a year later at 20 on the subject of municipal government. My dear family drove me down when Freshman registration rolled around and deposited me at Roble Hall which was to be my home for five years. Never will I forget the tears I shed when my family departed. I suppose I had never felt so alone in my life. But the sponsor in my corridor soon knocked at the door and took me to a movie and the coed life had started. I grew up at Stanford. I know I was truly privileged to attend. It was one of the country's great universities, and I shall set high value on what Stanford gave me as long as I live. To this day I make regular contributions to the University, hoping that all small gifts will help to keep this magnificent school alive.

Let us open the comments on Stanford with what is great about it. As I look back, the eternal lessons of the citizenship course required of all freshmen were perhaps the oustanding contribution. We were taught to examine all statements as to their ultimate truth. Whatever the subjects discussed, we were asked, "Is it true?" This lesson in objectivity is perhaps the greatest thing I learned at Stanford. Those unassuming, understated little section leaders who harped on this subject were perhaps Stanford's greatest attribute. The fact that they even existed is some kind of a compliment to Ray Lyman Wilbur and the intellectual climate upon which he insisted.

We were always asked: "What's for it?" "What's against it?"

And in those small sections of not over 30 students, we

examined diverse subjects. We were taught to be objective, to approach a subject in a spirit of detachment and objectivity. This lesson surely came through to me. If some of the social clichés did not measure up to the integrity of the philosophy which was preached to us, it was not the fault of those great little section leaders.

Independent study was another one of Stanford's greats in those days. If you qualified as a student, which by their measurements I had the good fortune to do, you were eligible for independent study. This meant you did not have to go to classes. There was an honor code which put you on your own to get your work done.

You reported on stated occasions to your faculty leader, who in my case was Professor Edwin Cottrell, a great educator if I ever saw one. Once a month I reported to him, and under his tutelage I produced a paper entitled, "The Allocation of Municipal Functions into Departments." On Sunday evenings he and his wife held at homes for the students in the political science department, and these sessions made you feel that you were an integral part of the University. What wonderful people they were! During my graduate year I did another paper under his guidance—this time "Taxation in California." It is a tribute to his detachment that I always thought he was a Republican. He told me later that he was actually a Democrat, but was trying to be impartial.

Stanford was very open politically in those days. Herbert Hoover was elected President, and my much admired Ray Lyman Wilbur was in his cabinet. But I was for Al Smith. We formed an Al Smith for President Club, and I remember that George Bodle, who later became very prominent in labor negotiations, was on the same team I was on to go to San Francisco and make a pitch on radio programs for Al Smith. We lost, but let it be said that Stanford never sat on us for deserting its favorite alumnus, Herbert Hoover.

Let me dwell a moment upon the fascination of the Farm. It was fun. We used to drive up to San Francisco. I had a friend who had a cut-down Ford roadster. We arrived at the Mark Hopkins to hear Griff Williams or Phil Harris, who had that entertaining song, "Let Me Take Off My Skin and Dance

Around In My Bones." At Big Game time we would go up to Berkeley, lunch at the International House or the Pi Phi House before getting into a frenzy at the game. By the time my beautiful nieces arrived at Stanford 20 years later, many students wouldn't even go to a football game. Society is far more affluent now, and we are asking for a different set of values.

Having mentioned some of Stanford's great intellectual qualities, let me now mention what was among her failings—her social artificiality. The sorority system represented some of the most barbaric and false values in our society; it was finally thrown out. It was to the great detriment of Stanford that it was done at such great human cost, and when it was finally accomplished some of the false values of the system seemed to surface in the self-perpetuating Board of Trustees and a later administration. Their hand was forced by factions they attempted to discredit and perhaps they overreacted.

I served for four years on the Executive Board of the Stanford Alumni Association. An alumni board is supposed to serve as an expression of open alumni opinion and to prevent the University from coming under the domination of an arbitrary and blind leadership. The alumni failed sometimes to accomplish this. In my opinion radicals and ultra-conservatives are both guilty of tyranny and they destroy the great magnanimity of spirit of those who are truly broad.

I love Stanford and what she has contributed. I still make my contributions to Stanford's budget; many of my fellows no longer do. I shall be happy to see an improved balance between good behavior and intellectual and social flexibility.

Stanford had style and class when I was there. She also enjoyed discipline and brilliant intellectual contributions. It is still a beautiful University; there are a gallant new president, a spirited alumni group, and a student body which numbers many earnest and charming young people. Admission to Stanford is a prized goal. Is it being awarded to the truly deserving? Many question this. Let us hope that the University's great attributes can provide a real education and make a contribution to the standards of an enlightened civilization. Hopefully excellence will be retained as a goal.

Mrs. O.H. Ritter, mother of writer, taken with infant son, Irving Ritter, in garden of home in Shanghai, China.

Mrs. O.H. Ritter, mother of writer, taken with infant son, Ovid H. Ritter, Jr.

Childhood Picture of Writer.

Childhood Picture of Writer.

Family group taken about 1917, in Hong Kong.
Reading left to right: Ovid Ritter, Jr., Mrs. Ovid Ritter with daughter
Margaret on lap, Lucy Ritter, Mr. O.H. Ritter standing, and Irving
Ritter.

Ritter children in Fourth of July parade in Hong Kong about 1918.

Mrs. Ovid H. Ritter, mother of writer, taken in Stockton, California, about 1941.

Mr. O.H. Ritter, father of writer, taken in Stockton about 1941. He was at that time Executive Vice President and Comptroller of College of Pacific, now known as University of Pacific.

Family picture taken in garden of Ritter family residence in Stockton, California about 1942.

Back row standing, from left to right:
   Irving Ritter, Ovid Ritter, Margaret Ritter (now Mrs. Arthur Frantz).

Front row, seated from left to right:
   Mrs. Irving Ritter with daughter Lucianne on lap (now Mrs. N.R. McIntyre)
   Mrs. Ovid H. Ritter, Jr. with son Michael on lap
   Miss Lucy E. Ritter
   Mrs. O.H. Ritter
   Mrs. C.M. Ritter, mother of O.H. Ritter
   O.H. Ritter

UNIVERSITY OF PACIFIC

MY FATHER in his later years became comptroller and financial vice-president of the then College of Pacific in Stockton—now known as the University of Pacific. He spent some 25 years there, and among other accomplishments created an undergraduate school of business. He believed that many young people needed a business education but did not have the means to attend graduate school. The success of this venture was indicated by the fact that this department soon had the largest enrollment in the school.

The saga of my parents' 25 years at Pacific is a chapter on the preservation of a college during unprecedented financial strains. Pacific, the oldest University in California, was originally domiciled in San Jose. It was decided, correctly in my opinion, that there was a greater need for a college in Stockton, which did not have nearby universities as did San Jose. A financial drive was carried out and pledges secured to move the campus to Stockton.

At this time my father, then a Stockton banker, was engaged to become the comptroller and manage the financial planning. He started this position with an attractive contract and high hopes; before his tenure there came to a close the Depression precipitated near calamity. There were drastic salary cuts and ultimately there was a period when Dr. Knoles, the president, and my father didn't even draw a salary—in order to keep the college open. There was a time when everyone but my father was ready to give up, but Daddy wouldn't quit. When students had no money he accepted tuition in kind—wheat from farmers' children, asphalt from contractors' children, services from gardeners and whatever else he could use.

My beautiful mother had one dress which she wore to all the college affairs, but she never faltered in supporting my father's determination to keep the college open. They both believed that you should never abandon a young person—that young people mature at different ages, and they saw Pacific through its moment of trial. They went to all sorts of lengths to provide jobs for young people, at the same time insisting that the young people recognize their obligation to the college.

All these years my father was teaching foreign aid and ocean transportation and money and banking and accounting, and my mother acted as a patroness at many college functions. And always our old chow dog strolled through the college halls and walked into the classrooms where he heard my father lecturing. The grounds of the campus were particularly beautiful; there was a great old Italian gardener named Bava, and he and my father discussed the camellias; and their gardens were among the showplaces of Stockton. A particularly notable achievement at this time was the contruction of Morris Chapel—a beautiful little chapel with exquisite stained glass windows. This became a particular project of my father's and he wrote a book describing the heraldry and symbolism of this exquisite little church.

Pacific has grown tremendously; it has been a very successful college and their recently deceased president, Robert Burns, introduced the cluster system into this country. This was patterned after Oxford in England. Whether it was the cluster system or a more relaxed valley climate or particular qualities of the administration, there have been no riots at Pacific. Discipline has been maintained, and the Central Valley can boast of a very popular, successful privately operated university. It practices some very original educational ideas and is an institution of which its supporters may be very proud.

My own dear parents lived out their lives at the school. My mother died suddenly of a heart attack in 1943, and I shall always remember the great wreath of camellias grown on the campus which graced her funeral.

Dear Daddy survived until 1959 and at his final services both Dr. Knoles, the retired president, and Dr. Burns, the then president, paid tribute to his contribution. The services took place at the beautiful Morris Chapel which he had created, with the stained glass window commemorated to my mother a silent witness.

Years later a dormitory was christened Ritter House in their honor, and may the spirit of their idealism be felt by the young people privileged to live there. They always gave more than they asked, and the world is richer because they lived.

EARLY BUSINESS CAREER

AND NOW comes my own career. In 1931 I received my master's degree from Stanford. I was fortunate to be a research assistant in the political science department and this paid my graduate tuition. A graduate scholarship I won paid most of my living expenses and a summer job helped with my clothes and spending money. My graduate year was a serious one. I knew I was to earn my living the next year and was anxious to prepare myself. The deepening Depression was making itself felt. Picnics and boating on the campus were simple pleasures. Dances in the basketball pavilion were notable events, and trips to San Francisco red letter occasions. We ate hot dogs for lunch so we could splurge at dinner and we viewed our chosen theater in 50-cent seats in the gallery of the old Curran. Came the awarding of degrees—a *cum laude* recognition—packing my possessions into my old Model-A Ford, and returning to Stockton to seek my fortune.

There seemed to be no jobs. And we had to work. Pacific's salaries had reached the vanishing point. We had long family discussions and in my timidity I was terrified of applying for jobs, but I did. My brother Ovid landed one at the Port of Stockton and I found one with the California Taxpayers Association, on condition that I helped to sell memberships in the Taxpayers Association so there would be money to pay my salary.

I wrote a paper recommending the consolidation of the city and county assessors and tax collecting offices. These recommendations were publicized and applauded, but some 40 years later we are still talking about the same reforms and not acting. I was paid $65 a month for my efforts.

These were happy days in many ways. I had my young friends who took me to dinner and cocktail parties. I belonged to a bridge club, but there were no raises. Saving was hard, and there was the restlessness of one 21 years old who wants to achieve and had to practice patience instead. Trips were out of the question then unless one inherited funds. I wonder if the young people who find it so easy to travel now ever count their blessings. I learned to do cross stitching and embroidery.

The young man I dated most often was as poor as I, and for those whose families could not supply them with funds, marriage was out of the question. It is quite understandable that the birthrate then was the lowest in the country's history. It would not have occurred to any of us to get married if we could not pay our bills. Accepting charity was not even considered as an alternative. If you couldn't afford or didn't intend to take care of your children, you did not have them.

The excesses of the hippy movement were not a problem in those days. The most far out episode I can remember then was a trial in which a number of my contemporaries were involved. They were accused of Communist sympathies. One of these girls was sister of one of Stockton's leading bankers. They were judged to be in contempt of court because they refused to testify.

Then there was a night when my brothers came home with the startling news that the American Legion was marching en masse down El Dorado St. to break up a Communist meeting downtown. This they did, and we drove down later to see what was happening. The Legion had wrecked the Communists' meeting room and thrown the bits of ruined furniture out the window. Scattered table legs and piano legs in the lot beside the building were mute evidence of the commotion which had taken place.

The Ritters took no part in such activities, as we had been taught that if we wished to express ourselves there was a legal way to do it, and discipline was a part of our upbringing. We were encouraged to become interested in politics however. I remember during this period accompanying my father to political rallies in the Court House Square where the candidates addressed the voters. I was most impressed when my father would occasionally go up to the candidates at the close of the rally and promise them his vote.

There was political ferment developing in those days. As the Depression deepened there was widespread discouragement with what seemed to many Hoover's lack of a program. The Hoover-Roosevelt contest, as I think back about it, was as much a difference in psychological approach as anything. Hoover was a shy reserved man who urged patience and fortitude. Roosevelt was a man of great personal charm who proclaimed to the people in ringing tones that "The only thing we have to fear is fear itself." So with his attitude of "Let's go," the people followed—not being too sure perhaps what they were all going to do, but convinced that they had to do something. And here was a Pied Piper who was willing to lead the way.

Roosevelt probably did more than any other one person to mold political thinking in this country. He produced something of a revolution in the political thinking by insisting that the government had a responsibility to keep a viable economy operating. Prior to Roosevelt, at least since the Civil War, the *laissez faire* philosphy had predominated—and it was generally assumed that business, if left to its own devices, would ultimately work through most dilemmas. I supported Roosevelt, and the size of his initial victories reflected the strong feeling on the part of the majority that something had to be done.

Looking back with the vantage point of 40 years one realizes that part of the problem of those days was that the country was coming to grips with the fact that finally we had pushed our Western boundary to the Pacific Coast, and the westward movement was over in that pioneers who didn't like the way things were run at home could no longer push out into the wilderness. It is true that the westward movement of capital and political power is still taking place, but this sort of movement takes place within the system. Formerly the individual who had difficulty adjusting to society could get away from it all. Our society has lost that safety valve. In its place we began clothing our politicians with virtues or crimes for which they were only in part responsible. They are in effect riding the crest of a wave.

I make this point here because 40 years later one realizes that neither Hoover nor Roosevelt was possessed of the extreme attributes attributed to each man in the spirited days of the campaign. They were both men who had been reared in some of the best traditions of our country. Hoover had been a great organizer and humanitarian, but he lacked the warmth and imagination a country needs in its statesmen at times of crisis. Roosevelt had the charm and imagination and political magic which the country yearned for in its hour of despair—so he became the Pied Piper to lead the people out of Depression. While it is popular today to downgrade him let us remember that he revived the country's spirit. He taught us to believe in ourselves again. Had we not had this revival, the country could have sunk into a far deeper morass than it did suffer. Many, many wise heads believed that the country couldn't take much more punishment. Roosevelt had the qualities which could stir a country.

He had a wife who became certainly one of the most deeply loved women in America. The sight of Eleanor, with her petticoat showing, putting on a miner's hat to go down into the mines to see what could be done touched this country's heart. The people recognized her great spirit. It may have taken us a long time to come around to this realization, but the imagination of the Roosevelts did help to restore equilibrium. In my opinion one of our problems today is lack of leadership which kindles the imagination.

I remained in the Stockton office of the Taxpayers' Association three and one-half years before their money ran out and the office was closed. My education and interest in politics had equipped me to do governmental research, but it was becoming increasingly apparent that organizations which depended on voluntary contributions had a hard time making it in the Depression. Certainly raises could not be considered.

I decided to go into business, for I was determined to have some money. The Depression was getting to me, and I knew I did not like the lack of independence which goes with no money. I regretted moving away from Stockton and my beloved family, but business opportunities seemed greater elsewhere. I remember our loyal old independent Stockton banker, Mr. Eugene Wilhoit (of a rare breed which has vanished), saying to me, "The trouble with you Ritters is that you all move away."

Alas! we had to. We all made more money.elsewhere.

Between my pleasant activities, including many long swims, I studied speedwriting. One of my swimming partners was Mary Louise Leistner, subsequently to become Mrs. Bill Corbus, whose husband is now vice-chairman of Great Atlantic and Pacific Tea. We used to go to Yosemite Lake and we swam out to a large war canoe at the mouth of the River.

I said goodby to this warmhearted existence, surrounded by friends and family, and accepted a job as a secretary for a year at Marin Junior College while I hunted for a job in business. This sort of work was definitely not for me. I wanted to do my own planning, and carrying out someone else's instructions did not appeal to me. So even the view of Mt. Tamalpais which all Marin County people enjoyed could not compensate for such (to me) uninteresting work.

I used my Saturdays to go job-hunting. This was a traumatic experience which I shall never forget, and which gave me a lifelong sympathy for working girls. I filed about 25 applications for jobs. I learned then that many businessmen were very kind and genuinely wanted to help all the young job seekers. But they could not do the impossible. Many businessmen did help me with suggestions as to places where I might try. A great difficulty at this time was that many organizations would not give any job, except clerical or routine, to a woman.

I well remember that when I filed an application I practically always got in to see the boss. My Stanford A.B. Degree did that for me. When I would walk past all the other applicants who couldn't even get an interview I had an ache in my heart for them. Never in our history had we had such vast numbers of unemployed.

I learned then to question a system that could wallow in such a terrible Depression. Human beings being what they are, perhaps there is no perfect answer. The drive and industry of each individual are probably his best key to recognition and always will be. Certainly the Russians do not have an answer with their system. I have visited in Leningrad and Moscow and Yalta and Odessa, and ridden through the great collective farms on the Red Arrow Express. To one raised with western standards, their life is pretty appalling.

Today's young hippies who don't want to work and exist primarily on family allowances certainly have no answers. They are only consumers and not producers.

Hard work and initiative still seem the best approach to the good life. In spite of a life cycle in which society developed a broad and humanitarian outlook which has unfortunately deteriorated on occasion into the excesses of civil rights activism, we are probably going to return to an era of survival of the fittest. A young person now, as when I was job hunting, who is willing to work very hard and live within his means can still make it. We must learn to understand what makes the system work and keep it on the track. One excess breeds another, and the excesses of the young activists may make everybody poorer and drive society into a more authoritarian regime.

Being in Marin County made it possible for me to go over to San Francisco on Saturdays and job hunt. People still worked on Saturdays in those days. One application I filed was at Wells Fargo Bank. I thought with my training in municipal government I would have the background to do municipal bond work.

Wells Fargo officers listened very kindly to my plea, but explained that the bank had an inviolate rule that women could not be on the professional staff and had to do the routine clerical work. However, they said that sometimes their clients came in and were looking for people with my qualifications, and they would recommend me should the occasion arise.

Will wonders never cease? Very shortly thereafter the vice-president and treasurer of California-Western States Life Insurance Company did go to Wells Fargo seeking a security analyst. Wells Fargo recommended me; an appointment was arranged; I landed the job and went to work for California-Western States Life as a security analyst at $110 a month on September 1, 1935.

I arrived in Sacramento with $1,100 in the bank and my fortune to seek. These 37 years later I am still there—as a senior officer in charge of the stock and bond portfolio of $200,000,000. I am writing this account as I enjoy a

51

beautiful cruise to the South Pacific. By the time I moved to Sacramento the Depression was lifting, but the clouds of World War II were darkening, and a new episode begins and a different set of problems.

SACRAMENTO

A BRIEF description of my own existence on $110 a month may help to explain the restlessness all over the country. If we were hard put to it to survive individually, this paucity was accentuated abroad and without doubt helps explain the willingness of the Germans and Japanese to listen to fanatics.

I lived in an old boardinghouse in a room without any heat. Room and breakfast cost $22.50 a month. I was so cold by the time I reached the breakfast table that my hands would be shaking. There was one upstairs bathroom and seven or eight used this in the morning. This meant arising very early in order to get to work on time. Dinner was not served in the boardinghouse, so I alternated between a nearby restaurant which served dinner for 50 cents and a grocery store counter where I could get a tuna sandwich and cup of coffee for a quarter. Occasionally I would treat myself to a weekend in San Francisco. There was a good commuter train at that time, and I walked all the way to the railroad station with my suitcase in order to save the quarter taxi fare. I was determined to save money and deposited $20 a month in a savings account.

The work at the office was very hard but interesting. We were building a portfolio in a growing company. Fortunately both the president and the vice-president developed a confidence in my work, so I had the satisfaction of feeling appreciated. One third of the bonds in the account were in default then compared to none now. This took a great deal of time, and I often worked weekends with no overtime pay. My company itself was working back from the edge of disaster and had to adopt rigorous measures for its own survival.

But life was not all bleak. The boardinghouse was full of other young college people working as social workers, Pacific

Telephone and Telegraph employees and State civil service people. We planned picnics after work and went swimming in the Sacramento River. That was considered very dangerous, but it did not cost any money.

I bought a car with the money I had accumulated from my former jobs and drove to Stockton often on weekends.

We played bridge in the evening, and took walks around beautiful Capitol Park which was across the street. At the end of one year of this rugged existence I was hospitalized with a bleeding stomach ulcer and was flat on my back in a hospital for three weeks waiting for it to heal, and then came three more weeks at home in Stockton with my parents while I was getting my blood count built up enough to return to work.

If life was hard for me, with my A.B. Degree at $110 a month, visualize what it was for the ones making $70 a month. We were all in it together, and if there was no disposition to violence or destruction in our civilized country, there was much discussion about the system and what could be done to improve it. This country was far too sound for anything like a revolution. But multiply our problems many times abroad and one understands the undercurrent of malaise which was sweeping over the rest of the world.

There were repeated accounts of the rise of Hitler in Germany—the hysterical paperhanger who seemed to mesmerize the masses with his histrionics. Mussolini was posturing in Italy, and there was a freeze on news from Russia as by now practically no one was getting in. The youth were marching in these foreign countries, and I well remember the atmosphere of impending doom.

The Depression was lifting here. Finally people were getting raises again. Unemployment was down, but there was all this awful news from abroad. The U.S.A. elected a leader in its time of trouble who appealed to the hope and courage in people. But the Germans and Italians chose charlatans who shouted about race hatred and greed.

Let us not forget this today. When it is popular to downgrade Roosevelt, remember how much better he was than what emerged in other countries, and that he spoke to high principles. We should keep this in mind for our nation must be making some choices today, which can be construc-

Writer on terrace of her high-rise apartment home in Sacramento (1967).

Writer in study of her apartment in Sacramento (1967)

Copy of photograph taken about 1958.

tive if mature, but can lead us to a debacle if immature. A great leader appeals to the good in people.

In these early working years vacations would be to Los Angeles, Riverside, Seattle and other nearby points. America was coming of age culturally, and tickets were purchased for the music series and theatre in San Francisco. The better off among us were now beginning to get married. The marriage age of our generation was one of the latest on record.

The company sent me on my first business trip to New York. This was arranged if I were willing to pay half the expenses, which I gladly did to have this golden opportunity. I called on other life insurance people in New York City, went to the top of the Empire State Building, and was invited for dinner at the Rainbow Room in Rockefeller Center. Can you imagine the excitement for a working girl to be having these wonderful experiences?

In 1939 there was a trip to Honolulu on the *Lurline* and *Matsonia*, and I stayed with my dear friends, the Eichelbergers. I had been maid of honor at their wedding and they had moved to Honolulu with American Factors. Subsequently, he rose to the presidency and chairman of the board of his company, and my company developed business interests in his company.

These early working years were pleasant, if somewhat uneventful. Limited funds kept our activities simple. Only the rich went to Europe.

My beloved parents were still alive and there were many weekends in Stockton. My brothers married lovely girls and soon had small families who brought joy to the hearts of all of us.

War clouds were gathering steadily, and suddenly there it was—Germany marched into Poland and World War II was upon us. It changed our lives and the World.

WORLD WAR II

THE FIRST part of the War was often referred to as a phony war. Major moves came slowly, as if the world could hardly believe what had happened. There had been such determination after World War I not to get into another such nightmare, and here it was all over again. Nations were not prepared for this new onslaught. It took time to mobilize.

I have so often thought if we had been able to avoid the Depression, World War II might never have materialized. War is often economic in origin. Poverty in the world provides a fertile breeding ground for incendiary tyrants.

The coming of the War created a new major dislocation for our generation. World War I and the Depression had been cataclysmic. World War II now came to remove whatever opportunities for normal development my age group had, for now we were in our 30's.

From 1939 to 1941 the war was gradually deepening but the U.S. did not get in until Pearl Harbor in December of 1941. It was a Sunday morning and I was home pressing clothes—a typical working girl's weekend chore—when the news came over the radio that the Japanese had bombed Pearl Harbor—a sneak attack that will be forever recorded in the annals of infamy.

This does not pretend to be a military account—only a delineation of the human tragedy of this holocaust and the disruption of the lives of millions of hardworking, peace-loving people who had no part in bringing on this war. Immediately after the Pearl Harbor bombing, Germany's Hitler declared war upon us, and the whole country dug in to win.

World War II was entirely unlike the Vietnam War. Most Americans have never understood why we were in the Vietnam War in the first place, but in World War II we were openly and brazenly attacked. Germany and Japan were out to conquer the world. They were soon joined by Italy. There was only one way to stop them and that was to fight back. There was no question in the minds of most Americans that this was a war of survival. The likes of the Battle of Britain would soon be in this country if we did not stop the enemy. We had to fight back and we did.

The men of my generation all became involved. One after another of my friends either was pressed into military service or had to go to work for a war industry. My older brother Ovid went into the Navy and became a Lieutenant Commander. He was assigned to the Port of San Francisco and participated in getting the vast quantities of war matériel shipped across the Pacific. My younger brother Irving, being by this time the father of two young children, went to work in a big shipbuilding concern in Stockton. A favorite bachelor friend of mine went into the Navy as a sailor and emerged a Lieutenant Commander. The husbands of my friends were signed up in one way or another. So life changed. The men were gone and the women were lonely. More than that, we were all deeply concerned about the safety of our loved ones. We had many early reverses, and it is hard now to remind one of the mental anguish and suffering of those days.

Because our manpower was limited, we organized the Waves and Wacs, the women's branches of the Navy and the Army.

I decided to join the Waves and spent many hours filling out forms and answering questions. The Waves had almost even decided on a special assignment for me teaching recruits at Smith College. Then the medical examiner ruled me out on account of my stomach ulcer history. I was bitterly disappointed and reminded the medical department that I had read that James Roosevelt had a stomach ulcer and was in the Navy. The Navy examiner snorted that James Roosevelt was the only man in the history of the Navy who had been accepted with a stomach ulcer, and his refusal to admit me was implacable.

I therefore stayed at my job and this too felt the war. Private investment slowed down to a walk, and we all bought War Bonds. Let it be remembered that the War Bonds yielded very little and most companies were in effect losing money by this investment, for the return was not adequate to meet corporate commitments. However, this was just one more burden of the War and we bought them anyway. It was unthinkable with all our boys at war that there should be any failure on our part to provide them with the proper equipment. And America was going all out. We went into debt at a rate that was absolutely incomprehensible to most of us, but we knew we had to do it. If the enemy won, everything would be confiscated. Gasoline was rationed, so we had very inadequate transportation. Shoes were rationed. Some of the dear older men gave up their shoe coupons so the children could have more shoes. Life took on a dull quality. The paucity of the Depression was back with us—this time accentuated by the additional fear for loved ones.

As always in periods of emergency, some of us were stronger than others of us. The more emotional members needed and received the counsel and comfort of the more stable.

I had a dear cousin who was in the thick of the siege at Midway and Wake from the very beginning. He was decorated and promoted as one of the youngest heroes. My aunt kept writing us how hard it was on him for one so young to see his friends daily losing their lives. He survived the War, with brilliance. He received great honors and accolades and then shot himself dead when it was all over. Being the youngest Lieutenant Colonel in the Marines could not assuage the terrible memories of the young men he had led into combat only to see them slaughtered.

National leaders emerged who won the love and respect of the people. Roosevelt, Eisenhower, Marshall, Bradley—these were names the people revered. They all had a certain simplicity, and the country trusted them. Without question, mistakes were made. Monday morning quarterbacks can always point out the errors, just as in the stock market you can always tell afterwards when you should have bought and sold. But these men were giving it everything they had.

There were terrible moments like Dunkirk, and the loss of battleships, but bit by bit our superior resources were wearing the enemy down. When hours were the darkest, there would Roosevelt be, suddenly showing up at Casablanca to show our boys we were all with them. Really he was a war casualty himself. He was getting thinner and thinner, and suddenly this country lost its wartime leader—at the 11th hour when the war was almost won.

The news came one afternoon when I was in the office. Our valiant imaginative leader, the only four-time President of the United States, suddenly collapsed and died. I do not think the country could have been more stunned. We had come to accept his leadership. Never before had I felt such a personal grief for one I did not know. I am sure a vast segment of the country felt the same way.

And beloved Eleanor Roosevelt said, simply, it was the whole country for whom she grieved in its hour of loss.

Harry Truman came in—perhaps not too well known at the time. But dauntless little "Give 'em hell, Harry" emerged as a strong leader in the best tradition of the country and will go down in history as one of the country's greats. He it was who had to make the momentous decision to drop the atomic bomb.

During the war years, on top of all the emergencies and strains a great research effort had been carried forward and at the conclusion nuclear power had been discovered. The whole operation had been kept very secret, but here we were suddenly possessed of the atomic bomb. And it brought the war to a speedy conclusion.

We had been bombing Japan like crazy at a staggering cost in human lives and human energy. Truman warned that we had a mysterious new weapon which we were going to use if Japan did not surrender.

Japan, the aggressor, refused to surrender, though every hour that the war lasted brought incalculable losses in human life and human misery.

So Truman ordered the first atomic bomb dropped over Nagasaki. The damage was incalculable and startled the whole world.

Still Japan did not surrender. The villainy of the Japanese war leaders decreed that there should be more young men slaughtered, so Truman ordered the second bomb dropped on Hiroshima with results that have become part of world history. It brought the Japanese to their knees and they sued for surrender.

There has been perpetual controversy as to whether Truman should have dropped the bomb. Of course he should have dropped it. We had been attacked, and every hour we stayed in meant more brave young Americans were slaughtered. The sinister Japanese leaders who started the War in the first place were the criminals. Their failure to heed our warning accentuated their callous disregard of the lives of their own people. The sentimentalists today who would criticize Truman's action are defending the ones who were guilty of the true infamy—the Japanese war leaders. It would be helpful if the sentimentalists and sob sisters would defend the people with courage and responsibility instead of making a maudlin display of their lack of common sense.

There is an old French saying, "A sinner can reform, but stupid is forever."

I well remember VJ Day. We were having an Executive Committee meeting in our office when the news was flashed to us. Mr. George Pollock, head of the Pollock Construction Co., which had built ships throughout the war stood up and turned to Mr. Peter Cook, Jr., a great agriculturist who had helped to keep food supplies coming.

George Pollock extended his hand to Peter Cook and said simply—"Congratulations, Peter. We have won the war." It was one citizen to another. There were tears in the eyes of all of us—and then silence. We all had our own quiet thoughts; gratitude that this awful nightmare was over and communion in our hearts for all the loved ones and valiant spirits who had been sacrificed.

PEACE

WITH THE coming of peace finally our generation could start to live. We had the problem of learning to live together on a peaceful basis, but this was something constructive. Now we could try to rebuild the world and reshape our own lives. The years from VJ Day in August of 1946 up through the early years of the 1960's were magnificent years in this country's history. The country entered into the reconstruction years with a great magnanimity of spirit.

Truman and Marshall hammered out the Marshall Plan in which for the first time in history on such a large scale the victor reached out his hand to help the vanquished. We sent money and aid to Europe to rebuild railroad stations and help the processes of capital construction get underway again. The Marshall Plan was basically conceived as an act of reconstruction and stimulus to growth rather than charity. If it deteriorated years later into a debilitating foreign aid program, that was not the fault of the original planners, but an indication of the mediocrity of later planners who were not wise enough to modify the program.

At the outset it was great, and not only helped to rebuild for our allies, but also acted as a great economic stimulus to our own country. Demobilization never brought the economic collapse some feared. There was such a monumental dearth of housing, roads, school buildings, automobiles and capital goods of all sorts that a great period of business activity was commencing. We had practically 20 years of unprecedented prosperity in which the country came of age politically, culturally and businesswise. Let us look at some of the developments.

REVIVING BUSINESS

DURING this period I had stayed in the same job, gradually advancing from the post of security analyst to vice-president in charge of a portfolio of $200,000,000. In this capacity I had an opportunity to study many facets of the business world, and to become aware of its great advances. The stock market is a reflection of the hopes and fears of business. After the war it was flat on its face. War and Depression had beaten it down to a pulp. Now was the golden opportunity to get in. The hardy souls who moved into the stock market in those years made a fortune, and many who did will be rich for the rest of their lives. Successful business and inflation changed the dollar price of stocks so spectacularly in that 20-year run that it is not possible for prices to revert to their 1948 level short of the bankruptcy of the system. The people who did their principal stock investing in that period are the ones who made money—not the performance operators of the late 60's.

It was my good fortune to be in the right place at the right time, and I did put the bulk of my savings into the stock market. The company had an Executive Committee composed of some very astute businessmen, and they too were willing to invest in American business; and my company embarked on a much heavier stock purchase program than was typical of the life insurance industry. The stock market program was one of our most controversial undertakings. How often our most remunerative activities are the ones undertaken before the crowd sees the opportunities!

We had on our committee Mr. Peter Cook, Jr., a man of unquestioned financial integrity who also had great imagination. He always stressed having a flexible approach. He was very articulate in urging that the company buy common stocks and he had the strength and weight to insist upon the acceptance of his ideas. Mr. George Pollock also urged the common stock program, and they were subsequently joined by Mr. David Wasserman. These three men were three of Sacramento's most enterprising and successful entrepreneurs, and the company was fortunate in having them on the Board. I in turn was fortunate in having their support. They asked me to pick the stocks. We had fascinating discussions about the individual names, and they hardly ever turned me down. I also had the stalwart support of my great old friend, Arthur Luddy.

As one of our most successful salesmen he was not on the Board, but his charm and sparkle and very bright mind and great integrity had won him a big following in Sacramento. He kept telling people I was making more money for the company than any other one person. With this kind of backing we had what it takes to make a program succeed.

There were many greats in this business at that time. Let me mention some of them. There was Russell Kent who ran the investment department for the Bank of America. A small man in physical stature he had the mind of a giant and the disposition of a saint. Besides this he was a great Democrat and was always telling me which of the Democratic leaders he admired most and what was good about them. At that time Russell Kent was running the investments for Occidental Life Insurance Co. also and shared his wide knowledge with me. He always had time for me. When you were waiting to see Russell Kent you might be waiting in line with a file clerk or the President of the World Bank. He found time for us all.

Then there was Mr. Jo Morris at First National City Bank—a delightful character. He urged me to buy General Motors long before it became a blue chip. He said it would finally become respectable and be on everybody's list. How right he was!

Once when he was urging me on a particularly debatable stock I said to him, "But Mr. Morris, you don't understand. I have such differences of opinion on my Executive Committee. I don't know if I can get them to agree."

He drew himself up and practically thundered at me: "Miss Ritter, what makes you think I don't have differences of opinion on my committee?"

He was a dear and helped our account to make money.

Then there was Mr. Leo Kane, also of First National City Bank. He was an expert on governments and a delightful and knowledgeable man.

One of the soundest in the business was Gilbert Colby. He was one of the most influential in the old Wells Fargo and was instrumental in shaping their policies. It is too bad they did not fully use his talents after the merger.

Jo Bickford, recently retired from Bankers' Trust, was one of the all time greats. He was more knowledgeable on bank stocks than almost any other advisor and, unlike many bankers, was willing to discuss them. He helped us to prosper in this area. He also had a vast knowledge of the people in the business and used it to help people out. In fact, he was known in the trade as Mr. Bankers' Trust.

These were men of vision and foresight, who contributed to the soundness and strength of American business—very different from the later day performance operators. A country or an institution is a reflection of the people in it. The success of business in the boom years had much to do with the strength of character and fundamental values of its business leaders. If we have strayed in more recent years we had better look to the quality of the men who are making the decisions.

Analysts in the early boom years based their choices upon fundamental values—sound asset position, true earnings growth, excellent management, strong competitive position in a vital industry. Later performance operators shifted with the crowd into fads and styles and look at the difference in the results.

Ironically the performance racket is linked by many to a Ford Foundation report. It took institutions to task for so-called uninspired investing and generally implied that they had become so hidebound and unimaginative that they had not done well by their clients. This is certainly true to a degree. Institutions have to be governed more by some overall policies than do individuals; in fact, this is generally required by law. Therefore by the time institutions get around to acting the magic moment has passed.

I do not see how institutions are ever going to have the flexibility and success of a shrewd and sagacious individual.

The reaction to the Ford Foundation report I am sure produced results opposite from those which were originally intended.

Boards of directors urged their investment people to get with it, and big accounts started dividing up their pension funds among institutions based on so-called investment measurements, most of which were specious.

The so-called performance craze then developed. Apples and oranges were compared with a great appearance of wisdom, and hot shot operators who had been lucky gamblers were widely written up as financial wizards. You could not tell these smart alecks anything. It put a great emphasis on short term results, and many investment managers were then forced into unsound practices by top management demanding immediate results and instant wealth.

The terrible fallacy of all this escaped the investing public, or a large segment thereof. You cannot get blood out of a turnip.

The 60's did not have the market push of the 50's because the bloom was off the rose. The 50's found the market at bargain levels and the Dow Industrial Average moved from 200.13 at 12-31-49 to 673.36 at 12-31-59. In the 60's it moved only to 800.36 at 12-31-69 because the market was high enough when the decade started. Trees do not grow to the sky. The 50's provided the sort of opportunity that comes once in a lifetime. The ones who missed the boat in the 50's tried to create an opportunity by sleight of hand gambling in the 60's. But it was not there. The more recent investment opportunities in the market have been government 8s at par, top notch tax exempts on a 7 per cent basis, and a few true growth stocks.

The losses to many performance operators, both individually and institutionally, were staggering, and many accounts never will recover their losses. In retrospect, the ones who slowed down stock investing in the 60's and took advantage of some of the bargains in the bond market are the ones who did the best. Many people refused to take profits in the 60's because of the capital gains tax they would have had to pay. This was another fallacy. Tax considerations should not be the main factor in determining investment decisions for they lead the investor into a blind alley. There is no substitute for the fundamentals.

I have been and remain a fundamentalist. Fortunately for my own peace of mind I did lighten my own stock holdings very considerably in the 60's—paid my taxes and am in a nicely balanced position with good stocks I bought in the 50's (still at large profits) and an assortment of short bonds, government flower bonds, and tax exempts which represent the profits I froze.

The booming stock market of the 50's helped all business, for when people are making money in the market they are more likely to spend money, which in turn creates more building and spending.

It is interesting to note that during the Truman administration we were still creating wealth faster than we were spending. Our national product was growing faster than our debt. We could afford a lot of the developements we undertook because of the rate at which we were creating wealth. Figures available to the general public will support this statement. Sometime during the Eisenhower administration the balance started changing. We began to think we could do anything, but we are finding out to our own discomfiture today we are not miracle men; and we are killing the goose that laid the golden egg.

If this country does not return to some more sound economic practices than those in which we are now indulging we are headed for deeper trouble. This is what the stock market has been telling us. We will never control inflation if labor refuses to listen to reason. Any society has a limit to the number of non-producers it can support. The minorities, immigrants, labor, hippies, foreign aid recipients, and poor and government all want a bigger slice of the pie. The growth in government expenses during the Johnson and Nixon administrations has become absolutely insupportable.

There is a supreme irony in that a Republican administration, supposedly devoted to fiscal soundness, should be going into debt at a rate exceeding anything which this country has ever seen, short of the peak of World War II; and we obviously do not have that kind of emergency to justify our present excesses. The lack of national leadership is abysmal.

Are we going to go full circle? I have dwelt upon the financial markets because it is the facet of business with which I am the most familiar. It is paralleled in other areas. The American standard of living has brought a better life to more people than any other system previously devised, but it is now under pressure. Inflation is taking its toll of people at every level. Our life style rose in the 50's, stood still somewhere in the 60's and is now endangered; because obviously we are spending money we do not have and are not producing. The decline of the Puritan ethic of hard work and responsible spending did not hurt too much for a while, because of our immense accumulated backlog. But time is running out. Are we going to turn around before it is too late, or is the sand going to keep running through our fingers?

Before leaving the business area it is apropos to mention the space program. I heard this program discussed on Wall Street many times in the post-war years. Most of the men I knew supported it. There was general belief that the country needed something to offset the demobilization of war.

The space program seemed a perfect answer. It was basically constructive and held unknown future promise. It mobilized the popular imagination and helped to hold employment and business velocity at a high level. It was more dramatic than education or school building. It was recognized therefore by both business men and politicians that it would be easier to get the public to support large spending in this area than in something more humdrum. And large spending of some sort was necessary to absorb the demobilization of our military forces. It seems to me that this program is proving itself.

I have often thought of Glen's answer when someone was criticizing the program when he likened it to a baby and said, "What good is a baby?" It has fired human imagination, and the incredible accuracy of the calculations and successes of the moon trips have rekindled the country's faith in itself.

I happened to be in England shortly after the completion of our first moon landing, at a beautiful old country home. The English family spoke with great admiration of the American accomplishment. It brought home to me yet another facet of the worth of this program. We had completed something very difficult at a time when the world needed some accomplishments. That the U.S. had done this at a time when the world needed leadership helped to reinforce our place as a world great—a role difficult enough for any nation to play at any time. When there has been so much international bickering, the space program has been a specific accomplishment of great note. So, in addition to its scientific value, it was a stablilizing factor in our economy and a somewhat inspirational program in the great spectrum of world position.

Economic developments are more and more essentially joined with political moves, so any further comments on business will be related to the wide swinging political developments of this period.

To a person such as I whose life has been profoundly influenced by war and Depression it was only logical that I should become very much interested in politics, and a large part of my energy did flow into this area. I was by now more securely established in business, and my life pattern gave me the time for it.

My beautiful mother had died suddenly in 1943 and in later years my father became an invalid and I cared for him in Sacramento and later a rest home. So my frequent weekends in Stockton had ceased and my home base was now definitely Sacramento.

I had by now a very attractive small apartment, done by a most talented interior decorator, Jean Carter; a comfortable car; nice summer vacation trips, a wide circle of friends, and the time and position to revert to my early interest in politics. It was to become one of the most fascinating of activities, and like the stock market led me to identify with the stirring life of our times.

POLITICS

MY SYMPATHIES had early been with the Democratic party due to my upbringing. My father was a Democrat, and as a child I remember his dissertations about Woodrow Wilson, free trade, opportunities for the working people, the League of Nations and similar Democratic planks. My mother, I think, in her heart leaned to many Republican candidates, but she was far too loyal to her husband ever to offset her husband's vote, so generally she was rather silent on political matters. As a young adult sobered by the Depression it was most natural that I should seek in the Democratic program some hope and solution for our terrible dilemmas.

In Sacramento one of my most admired friends, Roman Catholic bachelor Arthur Luddy was an outspoken champion of Democratic causes. He was a man of sparkling wit and imagination and always gave me support in my Democratic leanings. He had started life as a poor boy and by his own efforts had made himself a rich man and had always retained his sympathy for the working people. He was a common sense Democrat, knowing that one had to combine sympathy for the underdog with industry and productivity. In our highly Republican company he was a major stockholder, and his support of me offset the suspicion with which some of our minor office holders regarded my political opinions.

Working women have suffered discrimination so long in opportunities for advancement, and their effort for recognition has been such an uphill fight that it was only natural that career women tended to be Democrats—the party that concerned itself with the underdog.

I first became active in politics when Adlai Stevenson ran for President the first time. I well remember the night of his first acceptance speech at the Democratic convention. I was visiting my wonderful friends, the Peter Cooks, at Lake

Tahoe. I stayed up long after the rest of the household had retired in order to listen to the acceptance speech. It stirred my soul, and I decided then that if this kind of man were willing to get into the maelstrom of politics I could do no less than get in and work for him. His ideals were so high, his goals so lofty, his speech so lucid and beautiful and his wit so sparkling that he represented everything I could desire in a politician and statesman. I joined the Sacramento Democratic Women's Club, and this was the beginning of a long association which has brought rewarding friendships, hard work, and a shared sense that together great steps could be accomplished.

Adlai Stevenson followed by John Kennedy brought politics to a very high level, a lofty elevation which has deteriorated since the advent of the hippies and the activist marchers, but more of that later.

The Sacramento Democratic Women's Club had two key people in it when I joined, and they have been stalwart members in all the ensuing years. One was Mrs. Ruth Sauze, a beautiful woman with a gracious manner, broad outlook, and magnanimous spirit that made her a born leader. She was happily married and her son was grown, so she had the time to contribute. She is a woman of high principles, and though she believed in party loyalty as all party workers must, she would never support anyone in whom she could not believe.

A second active member was Clarice Rodda, whose husband Al is a State Senator and has been for some time. Clarice Rodda shares her husband's high principles and uncompromising sense of honor. She has a sturdy devotion to duty and her simple and unassuming manner just naturally draws support to her. A school teacher before she was married, she has an educated mind and the self-discipline of a person who has worked.

With members like these, the Sacramento Democratic Women's Club has been a very high grade little organization over the years. It has played a key role in the major campaigns and I have been proud to be its sometime emissary.

My first real role was that of Alternate Delegate to the Democratic National Convention in 1956—the second time

Adlai Stevenson ran. I choose to dwell on this at some length because of its great contrast to the 1964 convention which I also attended as an Alternate Delegate. Ruth Sauze and Clarice Rodda asked if I would permit my name to be presented at the County Democratic caucus as a candidate for the delegation. The thought was very exciting to me, and I said I would like to discuss this first with my company. I brought this matter up with my executive officer who said he objected very much because this was a Republican company. I challenged this position and said I did not see how he could make such a statement, that a company is supposed to be non-political.

However, he did take the matter up with our house counsel and general counsel in my presence. After a great deal of discussion both counsels agreed that the company should not interfere with my desire to be a delegate, and that I should be permitted to follow my own wishes in the matter. Overruled, the executive officer said I could go ahead but to expect no support from him. Support from him was the last thing I expected anyway.

My affirmative answer was then given to Ruth Sauze; and so one Sunday afternoon when the Democratic caucus was being held in Woodland she and her son, Bud Sauze, (a delightful person of great determination) and I, accompanied by a lawyer drove over to the caucus.

It was much more of a contest than we had expected. Several other women's names were presented, and a lively competition developed. That dear Bud Sauze quickly sized up the situation and started moving around the hall button-holing delegates and getting their support for me.

I must confess to a little timidity in the whole matter, but will wonders never cease? When the votes were counted I had the most, so I became a member of the delegation. There were then a number of meetings, as is customary in political matters; and considerable public notice was given to the fact that I was the Democratic Women's Club's representative on the delegation.

The convention was to be held in the Stockyards of Chicago. We all paid our own way, and as I remember, $600 to defray the expenses of the convention. There was a campaign train. It was the old Santa Fe Chief, and we all collected in San Francisco to start our expedition. I remember that my friend Arthur Luddy took me down and saw that I was safely aboard.

The campaign train was a wonderful idea. It provided a great opportunity to become acquainted with other members of the delegations from all over the State. We naturally ate meals together and had a variety of informal discussions on the way, so we were already a team by the time we arrived in Chicago. We were all put up at the Morrison Hotel. Each State delegation was in one hotel. One learns quickly to roll with the punch at such gatherings. Things do not go on schedule very much at a party convention, because there are so many caucuses that meeting times for the regular sessions were constantly being changed. The lobby was full of people and notables milling about.

This was the first time I ever met John Kennedy. I had had breakfast one morning with Senator Rattigan and as we stepped out of the dining room who should step out of the elevator but John Kennedy. Rattigan told him a story of his brother Joe in the war, and John was happy to learn of it. We chatted a few minutes. John Kennedy was an earnest unassuming young man and at that meeting I knew I wanted to support him for something bigger later on. Although the lobby was full of people, the convention itself was very orderly.

I had my pass and my own regularly assigned seat which happened to be very close to Eleanor Roosevelt's, so I saw her every day. She had the sweetest smile and was much prettier than her pictures made her appear. Dear Eleanor Roosevelt—such a gentle queenly woman. My seat was also near the Kennedys' box and the good looking Kennedy women came in often. I ate quite a few of my meals in the convention cafeteria and Sam Rayburn came in often to eat. An old bachelor, he was generally accompanied by his sister. He was not a partying type at all.

How natural and plain a lot of these big name people were! It made one believe in the system even more.

Sixteen years have elapsed since that meeting, but notable impressions remain. I developed a lifelong respect for John

Moss, our Congressman, for the way he conducted himself at a civil rights caucus. He supported the party plank which had been hammered out by Eleanor Roosevelt and Harry Truman among others. A group whom I considered quite radical wanted a more liberal plank. They badgered John Moss and tried to make it appear that he was not for civil rights, which was totally false. John Moss can hold up under fire if anyone can. He is a real scrapper, and won his point there. I knew then that if I ever wanted anyone to champion a point actively I could not go wrong with John Moss. He has been an excellent representative over the years.

The Harrimans gave a reception at that convention. What a faithful man Averill Harriman has always been to his party! It was a beautiful reception. I remember being quite disgusted because two well-dressed women with Eisenhower buttons under their furs crashed the party and were boasting about it and laughing at their prowess. I remember thinking what horrible taste they had. Adlai Stevenson gave a reception for Eleanor Roosevelt. He was devoted to her, and it appealed to our sense of solidarity. It was so eminently right for them to be friends.

It was John Kennedy who placed Adlai Stevenson's name in nomination. He spoke beautifully and composed stirring prose. He was a spectacular in himself. And then there was Adlai's dramatic gesture in asking the Convention to choose the nominee for Vice President. I was for Kennedy, but the vote swung to Kefauver at the last moment. Such is politics. But it demonstrated Stevenson's desire not to dominate the Convention.

It was an emotion-filled meeting. The "Yellow Rose of Texas" was a sort of theme song and I never hear it played today without thinking back to that stirring meeting. What an exciting time it was! We had real leaders then—Adlai Stevenson, John Kennedy, Averill Harriman, Eleanor Roosevelt, Harry Truman. We really believed we were helping to make a better world.

I want to emphasize how orderly and polite everything was. I had only to present my pass at the door to be admitted. There were no problems getting a ride to or from the hotel to the meetings. Other delegates going to the

Stockyards would invite me to share their taxi or private car with them.

I particularly remember coming home one evening in a bus. It was crowded and I was standing. A discussion started in my area about future candidates and I said I would be for John Kennedy.

A young man from New England hopped up and said, "Young lady, if you are for John Kennedy, allow me to give you my seat."

I sat down in the proffered seat and everybody smiled. It was a happy, good natured crowd.

I remember one afternoon on the floor of the Convention Hall, Dave Garroway came by and asked if he could interview me. He asked me a number of questions about my reactions to the meeting, which of course were favorable. The interview was broadcast nationally, and many of my friends told me afterwards they had seen me on the national hookup.

I mention these little items because it was still a time when a single working girl could be chosen by Democratic processes and could go to the Convention unescorted in perfect safety. There was never any question about my seat being available for me.

I remember sitting next to a Democratic National Committeewoman one evening after midnight at a lunch counter stool. There had been many civil rights discussions. I said I could not understand why there should be such an issue because I saw no conflict between civil rights and the capitalistic system, and I thought we could have them both. This was her position too, and it was the sense of the meeting.

We were for the system. We were trying to choose broad articulate leaders who combined intelligence and common sense with a sense of duty to their country. We were proud of the leaders we were choosing, and it was a happy meeting.

It was an emotional meeting. Many times there were tears in my eyes, listening to the beautiful ideals and the stirring music. It was an open meeting. I was invited to all the California caucuses. Finally it all drew to a close; the platform was adopted; the candidates chosen; and that glorious voiced Mahalia Jackson sang the "Lord's Prayer" in tones that rolled through the giant auditorium and reverberated to the rafters.

It was true we lost the subsequent election. Probably no one could have beaten Eisenhower who was a loved national hero. But we were always proud of our candidate, and in years to come the beautiful words of Adlai Stevenson will ring clear and true. If we had listened more carefully as a nation we might have avoided some of the mistakes we have subsequently made.

I worked on the subsequent campaign and helped raise money. We never had many contributions from big businessmen, and we had to finance our efforts with $10 contributions and the like. Many working girls did participate in the effort. Adlai Stevenson came to Sacramento on a number of occasions. I remember one cocktail party for him at the Del Prado restaurant. When I shook hands with Adlai I told him he was a candidate of whom we could all be very proud. Arthur Luddy was standing beside me at the moment and said he was glad I had said that because Stevenson needed lots of encouragement.

But Eisenhower was elected. He was a good and decent man, but we were treated to four more years of platitudes when we needed something bigger.

There ensued a period when I was not too active in politics. I faced some severe problems with my health, and a profusely bleeding stomach ulcer required drastic surgery and the removal of most of my stomach. A long and difficult convalescence ensued combined with the serious illness of my father. I look back at those years and wonder sometimes how I ever survived. Of course I continued working, as I was dependent on my own endeavors and my dear father needed my help.

He had been so valiant in his vital years, and as a citizen had made a major contribution to this country in forgoing income in order to keep the College of Pacific open. Now at the end of his life he needed help, and I was determined he should have it. He was cared for with his own private room and bath and a nice little garden outside his room, and we tried to keep him comfortable.

The one thing that was going in my favor at this moment

was the stock market. I was beginning to make money in the great bull market which lasted from 1948 to 1968. It ultimately lifted me out of my very constrained financial position to a far more affluent state. Some of my profits at this time helped me with my manifold burdens and even helped make it possible for me to take a Mediterranean cruise when the doctor insisted that I take a respite.

But back to the political scene. The Democrats were active in the State of California politics too and put Edmund G. (Pat) Brown into the governorship. I was active in all campaigns and in fact was woman's chairman in the Sacramento area in his initial campaigns. I became very fond of the Brown family personally.

Brown was a very personal sort of Governor; he trusted people and appointed people he believed in. When they were successful he was personally jubilant and let them know of his confidence. When they failed him, he was deeply hurt. When one of his appointees was found guilty of a personal crime Brown demanded his resignation and considered it an affront to his entire administration. He honored me with an appointment to the Executive Board of the State Retirement Fund.

I served on this Board for nine years until Governor Reagan replaced me with a Republican. My particular responsibility on the Board was investments. The account grew to a 4½ billion dollar fund in those years—I believe the second largest in the United States.

It was a very well run department. A Board member could not help but learn a great deal in such a post. The openness of the meetings impressed me first with its wisdom. All meetings were open to the public. Tape recorded minutes of all meetings were kept so there could never be any juggling of the minutes. The head of the system was a man named Bill Payne, and he was the match of any executive I have ever seen in private business. Very bright and well informed, he was broad in his outlook and had an excellent philosophical understanding of what he was trying to do. The department was beautifully organized. Payne is a man of unimpeachable integrity.

The Chairman of the Board was Stanley Fowler, elected to

the Board by the State Employees themselves. He demonstrated a remarkable skill in handling questions at the meetings. He could get through a vast amount of detail and still have time for questions from the audience, which he always seemed able to handle with courtesy and tact and information on the tip of his tongue.

In a day when people tend to lose confidence in the system, it is well for the public to appreciate what a remarkable system the State Employees Retirement System is. In addition to running the system and the investments, the Executive Board sat as a hearing board and listened to appeals from any members who did not think their allowances were properly set. Studying these appeal cases took hours of time. It was a very hard-working board—a credit to the State and the electorate.

Pat Brown never at any time put any pressure on us to favor any particular people or groups. Since very substantial amounts were involved in both commissions and assets, this is a point worth noting. It was a clean operation.

Pat's wife, Bernice, is a beautiful woman and her good looking sister, May Bonnell, came to Sacramento to help out. She served as the Governor's appointment secretary. This was an astute move on Brown's part. May Bonnell was a person whose loyalty he could trust completely. She was at the same time very bright and politically savvy and had much to do with the high calibre maintained by the Brown administration.

Let it be said to Brown's credit that he kept taxes steady and got by without a material tax increase. It remained for his Republican successor, Ronald Reagan, to put through one of the biggest tax increases in the history of the State of California. Reagan failed to exert the type of personal leadership where he could stay in control of his program. For the most part Brown did stay in control. This is a point worth noting. Too often we fail to appreciate when we have a solid operation functioning.

Pat Brown created an advisory board of key department heads and appointees to discuss general state matters.

This board was presided over for the most part by Richard McGee, then the head of the Department of Corrections. A pro in his line, he was well nigh flawless. A man of high integrity and intelligence, he conducted the discussions with skill and perspicacity.

My brother, Irving Ritter, for many years business manager of San Quentin Prison, often commented on McGee's great value to the State.

This Board over which McGee was presiding officer had no real power, but it nevertheless made itself felt in may ways. It is regrettable that so many people who wanted to repudiate the system failed to appreciate what a well functioning administration we had.

When the State Teachers' Retirement Fund was reorganized, May Bonnell asked me to recommend someone for the required bank official's post. I recommended Julius Hammer, a vice president of Wells Fargo. He was appointed and has been reappointed by the Reagan administration, and is now chairman of that Board and doing a very good job.

California has not had a political machine. We have been remarkably fortunate in this regard. Most of the leading appointments were personally chosen. Brown's finance chairman, Hale Champion, now has a similar position at Harvard University. I am not close to the present administration so am not in a position to comment on its appointments.

I had, as mentioned, been a little inactive for a while due to health reasons and did not attend the Los Angeles Convention when John Kennedy was chosen the Presidential nominee. But I could not have been more delighted with the choice.

He seemed to me to have everything—brains, looks, integrity, youth. His war record was outstanding. And he was a fiscal conservative. This was a point not sufficiently recognized. With his exuberant enthusiasm and sparkling wit and high ideals, he was at the same time very responsible. He did get the country moving again and kept his administration financially sound. So when I was asked if I would serve as Women's Co-chairman of Citizens for Kennedy in my area of course I said yes. He was everything we wanted in a President and I went to work with heartfelt enthusiasm.

It was a very easy campaign to work on because the Kennedys were beautiful organizers. You always got an answer to your questions; you knew you were part of a team and there was a real program. We knew when the candidate was coming and could organize rallies. Prior to the convention he had come to Sacramento and my friend, Arthur Luddy, had organized a luncheon for him. We all visited with him that day and could really feel the charm of his personality first hand. He seemed such a slender young man. It made one feel protective toward him.

We organized money-raising meetings, and one such supper was at Georgeann Kraus's lovely home, and we had a good turn out. One of the most exciting events was the Kennedy train ride. He organized a campaign train which toured part of the country. A group of us rode a bus up to Marysville one day to meet the train and ride with Kennedy back to Sacramento. We all visited with him and had our pictures taken with him. Senator Henry Jackson was on the train and I had a particularly nice visit with him. Tom MacBride, Henry Moss, George Johnson and others were there that day, and it was full of excitement. We had organized a rally in Sacramento at the Southern Pacific station, and there was a huge crowd milling about as the train drew in to the station. I was up on the platform for a while with the candidate. No one thought in those days of anything like an assassination. He was very exposed, but it was a friendly crowd and the rally was a great success. Then we had a large banquet at the Palace Hotel in San Francisco. It was very dressy; everyone was happy; our handsome witty candidate outdid himself and one could sniff success in the air.

There was a quality of elegance to John Kennedy's campaign. How important that is! It was before the subsequent deterioration of our style had set in. We had a good press; were getting money; and there were the Kennedy-Nixon debates. I think Kennedy really won the election the night of the first debate. He made it. He had confidence and poise and wit and Nixon just did not. Wit is not a Republican attribute. And so, with all the religious issue stacked against him, he went on to win the election. The first Catholic to be elected President just had to have something, and he did. He seemed to represent the quintessence of the qualities of a civilized society. He had the young

The writer visits with Senator John Kennedy on the Kennedy campaign train in 1960.

people with him, for he was young in spirit. I have often thought that if Kennedy had lived we would never have had the problem with young people which we subsequently did. The young felt that a kindred spirit had been elected. He was well groomed and his hair, though full, was cut in Ivy League style. He combined the casual manner which the young people loved with the social conformity which the older people expected.

His glamorous wife Jackie became a pacesetter in the fashion world almost overnight, and even the daughters of Republicans were modeling their clothes after hers. There was verve in the way they lived. Democratic wives seem to be personalities in their own right, and Jackie on the way to the inauguration lived up to the role—she, in a smartly furred outfit with a cossack hat and boots; he in a top hat and long coat. They brought style and grace to the White House. America had come of age.

I treasure a file full of Kennedy memorabilia, for they really kept in touch with their team. I have a number of letters from John Kennedy, signed by him and a couple of Christmas cards from John and Jackie.

Election night was an exciting time. As early returns came in, which tended to favor Nixon, my friend, Arthur Luddy, and I made calls on various friends, Tom Sertich, Georgeann Kraus, Judge and Mrs. Finnegan. Then I joined Tom MacBride, men's co-chairman of the campaign, down at campaign headquarters and we served coffee and doughnuts. It was an exuberant evening, and crowds of well wishers kept milling about.

I did not go to the inauguration. After all, I am still a working girl. Although the party was generous with invitations and my friend, Arthur Luddy, did go, there was a terrible snowstorm which tied up a lot of people.

I decided that instead I would go to see Kennedy in the White House the next time I went East. This I did. An appointment was arranged for me through my Congressman John Moss and Presidential Aide Fred Dutton. I shall always remember that day. It was arranged that after a special White House tour I was to be directed to the office wing and ask for Mr. Dutton. This I did and he showed me around the executive offices.

Bobby Kennedy was there in his role of Attorney General, and Dutton and Bobby had their offices right near the President's.

There were a great many press people milling about as Kennedy was about to sign some important legislation.

There was a tiny little office just outside Kennedy's and there was Caroline Kennedy talking a blue streak to some of her father's secretaries. She was a beautiful exuberant child and she was obviously having the time of her life.

We went into Kennedy's office and a number of legislators were gathering because of their interest in the minimum wage legislation. We stayed in a few minutes and Kennedy chatted about the legislation and signed it. Then Fred Dutton took me out to the rose garden and we strolled around there.

I went on to be the guest of my Congressman John Moss for lunch. And in my heart I knew that democracy was still functioning if a working girl from Sacramento could be invited into the President's office in the White House in such a gracious manner.

A couple of times after that I saw Kennedy in Europe. Once my niece and I were stopping in Cologne, Germany, when the bellboy excitedly told us that our President was coming to Mass in their great cathedral the next morning. My niece, Nancy, and I went out and joined the throng which watched him enter the magnificent old church and shortly thereafter came out again. Nancy and I both remarked on the significance of our President's coming simply to pray with the Germans in their own beloved old cathedral. To a country where soldiers had come to fight so often, it was beautiful that our young President had come to pray.

I am sure that the point was not lost on the crowd of Germans who had gathered respectfully to watch him. I particularly remember a large German man shielding my niece and me from the surging crowd. He could tell we were Americans and spoke appreciatively to us about our President's visit.

A few days later my niece and I were in Frankfurt and there was Kennedy again. He was being driven through town on his way to make one of his famous speeches at the Frankfurt meeting house. He was riding on top of the car so everyone could see him and he was bowing and waving. A huge cheer welled out as he went by. What a marvelous messenger he was from America to the previously wartorn country!

In our own country two events particularly impressed me about him—his roll back of the steel price increase and his positive statement that this country would not devalue the dollar. The firmness with which he handled both issues really settled the questions at that time and showed who was boss. It is something we need in Presidents. A forceful personality can lead sometimes by suggestion as much as by law, and we have too often lacked recently an articulate President who could really lead by his personal stature and largeness of spirit. Probably Kennedy's greatest mistake was the Bay of

Pigs. He was quick to accept the blame for it, though actually there is evidence that in large part he was following a program developed by the previous administration. Had he lived, it is very likely that he would have developed a pretty skillful program in this area, for he was surely demonstrating a quality of toughness and sagacity in a variety of ways. This was evident in his handling of the missile crisis.

And then we lost our wonderful young knight. Did we not deserve him—that he should be so quickly taken from us? There will always remain doubts about what happened in Dallas—the black band on the newspaper the morning before the assassination—the hostility of some of the Texas people.

I have never been able to believe that it was one man acting alone. There was too much that was sinister about the people who wanted him removed. I have always thought that in some way a fascistic element made use of young Oswald to get Kennedy out of the way. We will never know the answer.

AFTER KENNEDY

THE STEVENSON and John Kennedy campaigns seemed to be the flowering of American democracy at its best. These two leaders were very special—far above the category of mediocrity from which it is the fate of democracy to choose most of its spokesmen.

Then came the Johnson campaign. I was asked if I would be chairman of this in our area. I said I would as I felt we should hold things together. After the terribly traumatic experience we had just been through the team needed to help bind the wound. Governor Pat Brown named me to be an Alternate Delegate to the Democratic National Convention to be held in Atlantic City, New Jersey. I accepted with pleasure. I am sure that some of my Catholic friends (I am an Episcopalian) urged that I be chosen. So 1964 found me going down to Atlantic City after a business trip to New York City. Once again we paid our own expenses and the California delegation was all housed in one hotel.

This time I knew many more people than I had known in 1956—Pat Brown, Jess Unruh, Libby Gatov, Bill Orrick, Dick Rodda from the *Sacramento Bee*, Ann Alanson. My cousin, Norman Ritter, from Curtis Publishing was there covering the convention as a reporter. My sister and her husband, Mr. and Mrs. Frantz, came down from New York for the opening, as I was able to get them passes and they were very much interested in the issues. The hotel seemed rather shabby and we met of course in a cloud of some gloom.

It was less than a year since our sparkling John Kennedy had been murdered; there were many who were uneasy about the manner in which Johnson had treated Bobby Kennedy and the mounting strain between them. Nevertheless the majority of delegates came in a businesslike manner and hoped to shape a reasonable program after a due period.

The first sign of trouble was all the young people milling

84

about. Precursors of the hippies, there were countless young girls in jeans, barefoot and with long hair streaming and boys who were equally casual. For all their seeming nonchalance, the similarity in their garb amounted practically to a uniform. They congregated in an area near the large pier, which was close to the Convention Hall. My first impression was of the docility of their behavior, for in the afternoon they were quiet and orderly but walking constantly in a circle around their gathering spot. In the evening at the first meeting we knew what we were in for.

When my sister and her husband and I started over to the meeting place it was practically impossible to get in. I did not realize at first what had happened. There seemed to be an impenetrable mob of people blocking the entrance. The usual "I beg your pardon" or "Pardon me" were of no avail. These people would not let you through and were beginning to get rough. My brother-in-law, sensing what was happening, told my sister and me he'd get us in one at a time. So my sister waited outside; he took me first, trying to explain that I was a delegate and had a pass. He put his arms around me and strong-armed our way through.

I thought my arm was going to be broken before we made it through, and my clothes were disheveled and pulled around. I had never been in such a situation before and felt speechless and horrified when we finally pushed, wormed and struggled our way into the hall.

Then my brother-in-law returned for my sister and went through the maelstrom again. If it had not been for his efforts I never would have made it in there. It was the first time at any political meeting I have attended that force had to be used to get in—a grim forewarning of the terrible trouble that was to break out in Chicago four years later.

After the evening session with its undertone of violence, my sister Margaret said, "I'm not leaving this place till we take Sister with us." And she meant it.

We had cots moved into my room. There were no extra rooms available by then, and they stayed till the convention was over and we all drove back to New York.

I was determined that the mob was not going to block my attendance, and my brother-in-law Arthur was equally determined that this disorderly band should not interfere with the proper functioning of a democratic society. It was the first time I had seen our destructive youth in action—the activists who came to block and hinder rather than to build and create.

Culminating a period of advancing civilization in which a single woman could sustain herself, these hoodlums in one ruthless action made it practically impossible for a single woman to attend as a delegate unless she had a bodyguard.

After the first meeting we were all warned that it would be advisable to go very early before the mobs expected us. This we did going as early as a couple of hours before the meeting so we could enter unmolested. You can imagine what this did to one's dinner hour. The meeting generally was not a satisfactory one to me. There were so many people milling around in the hall we were not sure we could get our seats back even if we loitered for only a few minutes.

It was, of course, a foregone conclusion that President Johnson would be our nominee; there was some suspense as to who the Vice Presidential candidate would be. Johnson did his best in an effort to develop drama and arouse interest in the candidate. He described his man in the most glowing possible terms and finally identified him as Humphrey. Humphrey had excellent Democratic credentials. Nevertheless many felt that he had compromised himself so much on the Vietnam war they were really not happy with him.

There was considerable bickering during the meeting about various issues, particularly the Negroes. One Negro delegation demanded to be recognized over the previously designated one. Such troublesome questions had to be answered one by one. It seemed sometimes as if we were spending so much time on publicity seeking antagonists that we never got around to the large issues and the uplifting ideals of a civilized society.

An undercurrent of dissatisfaction was present throughout because of the treatment accorded Bobby Kennedy. Many wanted him for the Vice Presidential candidate. Johnson did not. He would not permit Bobby Kennedy to appear till after the Vice Presidential candidate was selected—so that no possibility could exist that a sudden outburst of enthusiasm for him would suddenly make him the Vice Presidential candidate. So Johnson assigned the last evening to Bobby Kennedy—after the business of the convention had been completed.

It was the highlight of the whole meeting. The ovation when Bobby appeared went on and on. It was thunderous and from the heart. The love for his fallen brother, the outrage the delegates felt toward what they considered Johnson's shabby treatment of Bobby Kennedy; the sympathy for that doughty little figure—it was all there. Bobby stood high on the platform in the hall, a brave spare little figure; and time and again he tried to speak, but the tremendous emotional outburst went on and on and welled to the rafters of that huge hall. A terrible murder had denied the people of this country a sparkling leader and a responsive government, and the delegates weren't going to sit down till they had communicated their outrage to a listening country. Bobby and Ethel had been present during the Convention, and had come to breakfast one morning with the California delegation and we had all visited with them and shaken hands with them. Both had an unassuming unpretentious way and we felt that they were one of us.

Finally the hall subsided and Bobby talked. Bobby was tough, disciplined and highminded. He spoke beautifully. I still carry in my notebook a quotation from Robert Frost he used that night, "But I have promises to keep, and miles to go before I sleep."

He dedicated his life to the unfinished work of his brother. When he finished there was not a dry eye in the house. Democrats have a way of becoming very emotional and they rose to great heights that night. Johnson was the nominee, but it was Bobby's convention.

A highlight of our stay in Atlantic City was the Harriman reception for Jacqueline Kennedy. It was beautifully done. As the delegates arrived, we were individually greeted by beautiful chic hostesses (among them Mrs. Auchincloss) and led upstairs to the receiving line. There they all were: Bobby and Ethel, the Harrimans, Lady Bird Johnson, Eunice Shriver and Jacqueline. Jackie was beautiful. It was the first time I had met her. She had on a beautifully made quilted white dress; it was very simple; the detail was in the quilting. She wore no jewelry. Her dark hair and wide expressive eyes, contrasting with the simple white dress presented an atmosphere of elegance for the occasion. After we had gone down the receiving line we were ushered into a reception hall where Jackie soon came out and spoke to us. She thanked us all for taking the trouble to come. Actually, most of us would have dropped our eye teeth to get there. She said she had wanted to come because she wanted to say thank you to us all for what we had done to help John Fitzgerald Kennedy and that was all. Again the simplicity and beauty of the Kennedys had reduced us all to tears. I happened to be leaving the hall afterwards just when she was making her exit. She came out alone—a lonely quiet figure, and entered a waiting limousine. She so needed someone's love and protection. She is entitled to any happiness she can find. The traumatic experiences she went through would have felled a lesser woman, and a large part of the press in this country was absolutely sadistic toward her.

I like to remember the remark of the British paper which said after the funeral that Jacqueline Kennedy had brought nobility to this country.

And so the convention was over. My dear sister Margaret and her husband Arthur drove me back to New York. Camelot was behind us and we were entering a period when too many seemed to wish to reduce themselves and their country to the lowest common denominator.

Johnson kept stepping up the Vietnam War. From the very beginning I was opposed to it, and my friends will bear out my statement. It is one of the greatest disasters upon which we ever embarked. Johnson's advisors could not have studied history very carefully, for all history has taught us that no one can attack Orientals on their own soil in a guerrilla war and win. But the representatives of this country thought that they could defy history and they led this country down a self-destructive path before waking up. There was no moral or historical or logical justification for our role in Vietnam. We thought, under Johnson's stewardship, that we could afford guns and butter; and before we found out that we could not, we had in effect lost the war, created a vicious inflation, and downgraded the enlightened and constructive elements of our society.

The war was the tragedy of Johnson's administration and in the end it proved his undoing. Unquestionably it had much to do with his decision not to run again in 1968. There was much that Johnson did that was admirable. He made real headway in the area of civil rights, and certainly those with magnanimity of spirit could not resent some advancement for the blacks and other minorities. When the heat of the campaigns has finally subsided he will surely be remembered for his stature in this area.

We all pitched in and worked on the campaign. We knew that the country needed to be held together after the traumatic experience of the assassination. His opponent Goldwater antagonized so many, even in his own party, that the outcome was never really in doubt. A landslide kept Johnson in office, and Congress seemed to rush to approve all the legislation he requested. Perhaps Congress was having an attack of conscience about all the legislation it refused the fallen Kennedy; so Johnson did have a smooth time with Congress.

We had the usual dinners and campaign meetings. I remember Johnson coming to a banquet at the Hilton Hotel in San Francisco and a Sacramento contingent drove down to that.

I was honored with an appointment with President Johnson in the White House. I had been attending a Security Analysts meeting in Richmond and drove up to Washington with friends. On the appointed hour I arrived at the White House. I remember that Gregory Peck preceded me in the Presidential Suite, looking tall, handsome and relaxed. I was met by Marvin Watson and we had a pleasant chat in a small room outside the Oval office. A Steuben owl in there was a familiar note. Then we went in to see the President who was gracious and smiling. His dogs jumped all over me, but since I am very fond of dogs this did not bother me. In fact, it introduced a pleasant note of informality. The Oval office is a beautiful spot—with the famous rose garden visible through the glass doors.

The President seemed handsome and taller than his

The writer has an appointment with President Johnson in his office in the White House in 1965.

pictures—and this was just before his going to the hospital for surgery. A photographer came in and took a picture of me shaking hands with the President, and this is obviously a highly prized possession. I told him I would give him all the support I could.

There was so much that was polished and smooth and gracious about Johnson that it is a real tragedy that the Vietnam War overshadowed practically everything he did.

In my opinion the Vietnam War is one of the greatest blunders this country has ever made. Bit by bit it has almost torn the country apart. At the outset unfortunately I believe most Americans were for it, having accepted the domino theory. But as we bogged down further in its morass, building our troop occupation from 17,000 at the time of Kennedy's death, to over 500,000 at the peak; as the hopelessness of the campaign impressed itself upon more and more people, public opinion turned against it. The enormity of what we were inflicting upon the Vietnamese people became more apparent. At home the pangs of inflation were hurting more and more people. The youth of the country turned violently against a war whose motivation could not be explained. Fathers said they would support sons who refused their draft calls. There was an irony in all this as Johnson had run on an anti-war platform, and Goldwater had supported the war.

The military, against which Eisenhower had once warned us, must have exercised great influence over Johnson. In fact, it must also have affected Nixon, for here he is too, in the fourth year of his administration, having run on an anti-war campaign, and he is still in it.

Since war tends to be the hardest on economically depressed individuals the whole situation aggravated the minorities problem. Assorted minorities keep demanding special minority treatment. Hardly anyone speaks any more about being an American, unless it be the once maligned DAR who have emerged as a group who deserve some respect. Minorities have raised their voices with such cacaphonous demands that they will reduce the country to impotency if we let them all have their way. Some have forgetten that in order to share wealth it must be produced. Kennedy's admonition to ask what you could do for your country rather than what your country could do for you has seemingly been forgotten.

The political situation deteriorated steadily after Kennedy's assassination. A great support was building up for Bobby Kennedy. He was one of the few national leaders to whom youth would listen. In my opinion he was headed for the Presidency after his California victory, but a minority member's bullet cut him down too.

I remember a delightful meeting in Sacramento when Rose Kennedy came here to campaign for Bobby. I was privileged to meet her at the airport and introduced her at the luncheon we held for her. Valiant Rose Kennedy—I don't know how she has carried all her burdens. Her marvelous faith and courage, combined with her great sense of self-discipline have carried her along. I always remember how cute she was. In her 70's, she arrived in comfortable rather than stylish shoes. When photographers arrived to take a picture she begged a moment's delay while she changed her shoes. The next morning as the principal speaker at our meeting, she was modishly dressed to the last detail, including textured stockings. She expressed great interest in the campaign. Like any mother she said, "You know the reason I am here is to help Bobby."

But Bobby too was killed. In view of the terrible personal tragedy and the loss to the country as a whole, it is necessary to dwell upon how it hurt the Democratic party too. The Democrats had groomed the Kennedys for leadership. They wore their mantle superbly. The loss of both brothers in such a short space of time left the Democratic party without effective leadership. No one emerged who could hold all the factions together, and the party is becoming fractionated and splintered. Strong national leadership does not often emerge overnight. In view of the vacuum created in the Democratic party, leadership at the national level passed to the Republicans and Nixon. Nixon is writing his own record and will be judged by it. There are many who feel that his programs have contributed to the widespread social malaise and unrest.

In no area has he been more inept than the financial. His unprecedented deficits—$30 billion a year average for the first three years of his administration; compared to six billion a year for the preceding ten years—have shattered all records and triggered off an inflation that will destroy us all if it is not conquered. I stated earlier that economic troubles were often at the root of political disturbances—witness the Depression of the 30's building up Hitler and Mussolini. This inflation is contributing to the deterioration in our schools, highways and other justifiable programs while the monstrous and overwhelming welfare budgets overshadow everything productive. The Nixon game plan has been a disaster, but in the present state of disarray in the Democratic party we may have Nixon in office for some time to come.

The very strange decisions of the Warren Court, originally set up by Eisenhower, have only aggravated the situation. It is interesting to note that Kennedy's one appointee to the Supreme Court, Byron White, has consistently voted with the conservative minority in supporting the Constitution.

So at this disturbing political juncture I shall bring this political part of my memoirs to a close. Since Nixon and Reagan have been in office I have naturally not been personally involved in policy-making discussions and campaigns except at the local level. I shall continue to support Congressman Moss and State Senator Al Rodda, who are excellent men in the tradition of Adlai Stevenson and John Kennedy. I was on the steering committee in the Tunney campaign.

We live in such a great country that hopefully new leaders will emerge who will emphasize and dwell upon our points of strength rather than exaggerating our blemishes. As they develop let us hope that this country will recognize them and regain the equilibrium which it has come perilously close to losing in this period when we seem to wish to descend to the lowest common denominator rather than reaching for the stars, which has been our previous way. I shall help when and where I can, as the occasion arises. I was raised to believe that we should share political responsibility and contribute of ourselves in this endeavor.

Both major parties have played a role. This has been necessary and continues to be. The Republicans have contributed managerial ability and support of private business, which in turn has kept up the generation of capital so essential to the capitalistic system. The Democrats have contributed imagination and a belief in broad humanitarian principles which have helped to provide a broader income base and in this way they too have thus contributed to the creation of more capital. And unquestionably both major parties have believed in the American system.

As I spent less time in the political area, other activities emerged in the world of business and art and literature and let us talk about these.

TRAVELS

MY LIFE has been enriched throughout by my good fortune in being able to travel. Beginning with my first trip to Europe in 1948 with the Peter Cook family, my first major trip as an adult, I have had many subsequent trips, traveling sometimes with friends, sometimes alone. Success in both politics and business is enhanced by an understanding of what is happening in the rest of the world, and I am sure that both my investment activities and my political were more rewarding to me because of what I learned on my trips. And they have been such fun.

The first trips tended to be the most strenuous. One feels constrained to take in all the sightseeing possible on early expeditions. Repeat trips can be done in a more leisurely manner and two of my favorite repeat trips are to beautiful Paris and London. Surely England and France are two of the most truly civilized countries in the world. I never tire of strolling along the Victoria Embankment in London or going over to Trafalgar Square and watching the birds and the people, and admiring anew the great old lions. And beautiful Paris—the Champs Elysées with the Arc de Triomphe at one end and the Place de La Concorde at the other. Who could tire of that? Or having an *apéritif* in the soft twilight glow on a summer evening by Notre Dame—while the students of the world stroll by.

In 1953 I went around the world, again with my friends the Cooks and Arthur Luddy. That's when I saw the Taj Mahal, to me the most beautiful building in the whole world. We spent several days up in Darjeeling, with the magnificent Mt. Kanchenjunga in the Himalayas before us constantly. There we chatted with Sherpa Tenzing Norgay of Mt. Everest fame, a gracious charming man. I loved India. There is a gentle quality there. Monkeys and sacred cows wander everywhere, though people cannot really afford them. The

Mrs. Adolph Teichert, Jr. and Miss Lucy Ritter, taken on board the *Queen Elizabeth I*, en route from London to New York City in 1963.

Group taken in front of the Trevi Fountain in Rome in 1953.
From left to right: Mr. Arthur Luddy, Miss Lucy Ritter, Mr. Peter Cook, Jr., Miss Marion Cook (now Mrs. Tom Tilton), Mrs. Peter Cook, Jr.

boat ride down the Ganges River at Benares is one of the most unbelievable memories of my life. All those people sitting in the dirty water, lost in rapt contemplation—most assuredly it was not a Western scene.

There was the soft-spoken little boy in Bombay who approached me with his box and said, "Madame, would you like to have your corns removed?"

And the memory of all those people lying around the hotel doorway in Calcutta still haunts me. They lie in the gutters and doorways because they have no homes. Could anyone doubt the value of birth control clinics, after visiting India? It is a lesson and a warning to Americans against overpopulation.

I remember even then there were many signs about birth control clinics, sponsored by the more educated women of India.

Then we went down to Africa—into the depths of the continent and saw the most primitive people I have ever seen. Our first stop on the Comet Jet was Victoria Falls, one of the world's most magnificent sights, and then we took a boat ride down the Zambesi River and saw crocodiles swimming all about us.

I shall always remember my encounter with the native boy at the Livingston Hotel. I gave him some money to clean my shoes, after our expedition to the Falls. Both he and the money—along with the shoes—promptly disappeared, and I almost did not get them back before our departure, and then only because I personally made a search for them through the Hotel, and found them in a pantry. The little native boy could not have cared less, though he was quick to keep the money.

We went on to Johannesburg where the women slept with revolvers under their pillows on account of the race tension. Their native help moved their friends into the back gardens and expected them to be fed. Then we went on to the Kimberley diamond mines and Capetown. At Capetown we were warned not to go walking near the hotel. It was too dangerous. Then on to Durban, where a great massacre had just taken place—the Africans cutting down the Indians. It was said that you couldn't keep the Indians out of the

97

schools or the Africans in the schools. Next on to Kenya where we were openly insulted by the natives in the hotel. The Russians had promised every native a Chevrolet. We had not matched this promise, and though the Russians still had not produced, the natives were mad at the Americans. The fact that all along the line the animals were absolutely fascinating was overshadowed by the hatred and racial tensions.

Then we went on to the Belgian Congo, which I truly loved. The country was beautiful, and I remember the gentle native ladies saying to me in the morning; "*Bonjour, Mademoiselle, bonjour.*"

It was my favorite part of Africa. Here were the great elephant preserves, and to drive into a herd of 50 elephants with flapping ears, knowing that they could stampede your car if you annoyed them, was something to remember. We stopped at various resorts along beautiful Lake Kivu and spent many nights in the little rondavals. I remember that a group of European business men were traveling in Africa and that their route seemed to parallel ours. We had a number of visits with them. They believed strongly in educating the natives so that they would provide better markets.

Then we flew in to Ethiopia, the worst of our stops in Africa, the country where, according to the local pundits, the government lived on the income of the brothels owned by the queen (in addition to whatever they received from the Marshall Plan). Everything was disorganized and dirty, and the Emperor Haile Selassie the only connection with civilization. When I asked some people in the dining room what they would do if Haile Selassie died, they replied, "Get the first plane out of here."

Then we flew on to Aden, and I was happy to leave the racial tensions of Africa behind. In Aden everything was clean and efficient. Not even the sharks could bother us, for we swam in a reserve protected by wire netting.

We went on to Bangkok and viewed the exquisite temples which are a too ornate variation of the more sturdy Chinese art. Next Singapore—a sophisticated but not very beautiful city. A rough flight to Manila came next, via Saigon, and fun in Manila because we were entertained by Carlos Young and the Baldwins in his magnificent home in Manila, he a friend

Scene in Durban, South Africa in 1953.

Left to right: Durban Rickshaw Man, Mr. Peter Cook, Jr., Lucy Ritter, Marion Cook (now Mrs. Tom Tilton), Mrs. Peter Cook, Jr.

of my mother's from school days. Then back to my wonderful Hong Kong, the dream spot of my childhood. We stayed at the elegant Peninsula Hotel, and my family's fine old friends, the Maks, entertained us.

The senior Mr. Mak, in long gown, spoke to us through his daughter. This wise old Confucian had had his daughter educated at an English Christian college, and she was his interpreter. He placed his car and driver at our disposal, and his unmarried daughter was my special hostess. This was fitting, as I was my father's unmarried daughter. I loved these people.

The Chinese are among the brightest of the races, and being proud of their own race, they wish to remain separate and distinct. Intermarriage among Orientals and Caucasians was frowned upon by old-school Chinese, just as it was by us. I could write a volume about these stalwart sparkling people, but space does not suffice. I went on an island trip one day to an island in the harbor where my family had formerly had a summer home. Then, (in 1953), it had become a Communist fishing village, and was a far cry from what I remembered. In Hong Kong I walked around the Peak, which had been bombed, so did not recognize too much.

I want to go back to Hong Kong again, the jewel of the China Sea.

Japan and the exquisite Inland Sea I have visited on a number of occasions.

My most recent trip was a cruise of the South Pacific. I loved this. Tahiti is a place to which I would like to return. Relaxed and smart, with all the style of the French, I could go back here and settle down for a protracted stay.

Then on to New Zealand, which is so like the U.S. in its friendliness and general life style. It's clean and efficient, and a good adjustment has been reached with their native group, the Maoris, who are among the brightest of all the native groups. They are accepted, serve in the legislature, and obviously have developed a culture of their own. The carvings in their museum are truly worthy of note, and it is they who wrote that charming melody—"Now has come the hour when we must say goodbye."

On to Australia—bright, clean, attractive, with that tantalizing new opera house still to be opened, and their world famous koala bears. It is a country that generates little or no capital; so on its own it develops at a slower pace than one might expect.

Then there is friendly Fiji, really reformed by the missionaries who found cannibalism still being practiced as recently as the 1890's, and American Samoa, an altogether charming spot. What delights these South Pacific ports offer!

There was also a cruise to South America. São Paulo was the most fascinating of cities, perhaps because I could see it through the eyes of a wealthy and cultured Brazilian family who entertained me in their elegant white marble home. I never fail to remember my beautiful hostess worrying that because of the weak central government she could never leave her daughters alone for fear of kidnappers. She knew that this would weaken their sense of independence and was not a proper way to rear young people. Rio was beautiful, and I loved the beaches. I remember the furs in Montevideo, and that the wife of a Republican Congressman was bringing in half a dozen fur coats duty free (Congressional immunity for relatives, she said). Caribbean ports are fun, and a nearby favorite is Bermuda. I'd really like to go back there.

There have been many trips to Europe, perhaps the most fascinating of all journeys, for it is certainly the seat of our culture, and therefore close to our hearts. From the North Cape through the beautiful fjords of Norway, the lilting lightheartedness of the Danes, one could retrace many steps. When Hitler threatened the Danes for harboring Jewish children during World War II and ordered that all Jews in Denmark must wear a Star of David, every Dane in the land wore a Star of David.

And then there is tragic Russia. When the women don't care what they look like, you know something has happened. I had a warmth in my heart for many of the Russian people, especially the older women, but that government! And for all that posturing, the only things they have to show off, with the exception of the subway and the new Bolshoi Theatre in Moscow, seem to be pre-revolution. The stench was so terrible in their Gum store I could hardly wait to get out of there. The dead hand of dictatorship to require every visitor to stand in line for hours in the Red Square to file by Lenin's embalmed body is a ghoulish demonstration. Russia is full of beauty, nevertheless. They appreciate the spectacular collection of the Hermitage, and make it available for all to see. The unbelievable church in Leningrad with pillars of malachite and lapis lazuli staggers one's sense of reality. The talent and artistic imagination of the Russians are tremendous. How tragic that they have never seemed to be able to govern themselves well! For all their beautiful ballet and space development, the quality of their life is dreadful. I read *Dr. Zhivago*—as have many Americans—and reflected upon the tragedies it depicted. Those who sympathized with the Revolution in the early days, sensing the inadequacies of the Czarist regime were destroyed too as the Revolution proceeded on its cruel and bloody way. The country is finally opening up again, but it has a long way to go. The people don't smile; there is little of what we call freedom; living conditions are appalling, and the country just lacks the style and the dash of the free world. As a young woman I read many Russian novels; the imagination and the brilliance of the Russians have always interested me. The more is the shame that their inability to govern themselves has been so disastrous.

Europe is the continent that is the closest to the hearts of most Americans, for our hertigage stems from there. We tend to identify with what we see there, for it is a part of our family background. With my English, Irish, and Danish blood lines, I feel almost as if I were coming home when I visit there. English theatre is stimulating, and I was raised on Shakespearean quotations; "The friends thou hast, and their adoption tried, grapple them to thy soul with hoops of steel;" "The quality of mercy is not strained; it droppeth as the gentle rain from heaven upon the earth beneath." Another mentor was Browning who wrote: "We fall to rise—are baffled to fight better—sleep to wake."

England knows how to treasure her past, and a recent driving trip through England included a remarkable rendition of *Troilus and Cressida* in an open air amphitheatre overlooking the Atlantic Ocean on the Cornwall coast; and Stratford-on-Avon, with dinner overlooking the Avon River, gives you Shakespeare in matchless taste. The historic towns of Chester and Bath with their distinctive Tudor and Georgian architecture are full of history.

And then one thinks of the château country along the Loire in France and the beautiful drive along the Marne Valley where memories of Château Thierry, Belleau Wood and Rheims Cathedral make it hard to keep back the tears.

England and France have developed some of the finest hotels in the world. I just have to mention the rooms at the Savoy, with their beautiful view of the busy Thames, Big Ben, the houses of Parliament and Cleopatra's Needle. The elegant decors of the Savoy rooms leaves nothing to be desired. And in Paris there is the Ritz, with its lovely gardens, where one can dine out in the open with soft music, the fountains in the background, the flowering trees all about, and service that is unsurpassed. And in a day that is

Snapped during drive to Alaska on the Alaska Highway, August, 1962, with sister and brother-in-law, Mr. and Mrs. Arthur Frantz.

now past, perhaps a glimpse of darling Coco Chanel having her repast.

There's adorable Holland with the charm of the towns of Delft and The Hague, and great museums and art galleries in Amsterdam. To think about these now is almost to make me want to abandon working and go traveling again before it is too late. A boat trip down the Rhine is a must to see all those fascinating old medieval castles; and to visit in Bavarian Germany is to love it. This is not where the Prussians orginated.

The Mediterranean calls again and again, Cannes, Nice, Venice, Dubrovnik, Naples, and then the lovely Arabian cities of Tunis, Tangiers and Casablanca. Damascus is one of my favorites of all. Being away from the coast more of the old, old civilization is preserved unchanged, but it comes face to face with the modern economy of the oil world. See it for yourself on the Street Called Straight. Ancient people and modern ones are all there together. Damascus I would like to revisit. I just need more years.

And to jump a long way away, one of the most fascinating of trips was the drive to Alaska. My sister and her husband and I did this one, meeting once in Seattle and taking that long trek across Canada and the Yukon and into friendly Anchorage and boisterous Fairbanks and driving North from there on up to the Arctic Circle—clean, bright, friendly and beautiful country.

Many detailed travel books have been written, which this does not purport to be. What is appropriate to say is that there is beauty all over the world. There is love all over the world. It is hard to fight a country where you have visited and made friends. Civilized standards prevail in most of the world; not everywhere, but respect for human beings is spreading.

Someone has said in a facetious vein that the secret of civilization is plumbing. It is surely easier to live in an uplifting manner when living conditions are acceptable. But it has to be in the hearts of people to lift themselves. I never forgot some fine new housing which had been built in South Africa, but the natives who moved in desecrated the place with their own filth. And fathers in Africa sell their daughters to provide a living for themselves. People cannot blame others for their inadequacies. Most of us have to accept some responsibility for what we are. As we travel we can copy the best of what we see.

Overpopulation is surely one of the world's greatest burdens. Birth control can help to improve the standard of living and avoid the brutalizing of human values which accompanies children whose parents do not support them. Planned Parenthood is one of this country's more constructive organizations. Money spent to help this work will tend to mean less is needed for more conventional charities.

It is interesting to see how the prosperity of most countries in the world has improved steadily since World War II. Nowhere is the contrast greater than in Hamburg. When I first saw Hamburg it was a pile of rubble—from World War II bombing—with beautiful blond children playing in the ruins. Today it is an elegant, clean, sophisticated city.

Over most of the world conditions have improved and can improve further. Much will depend upon the common sense of the people. Human beings must produce in order to live well. The have-not nations do not produce enough to live as well as the more productive nations. The people in Hamburg lifted themselves. The people in other countries can do likewise if they will just do it. It is not enough to demand help from others, though the U.S. has been very generous.

My generation was raised to believe that God helps those who help themselves. This is still true. The extent to which world civilization can be improved will depend in large measure upon the hopes, aspirations and industry of the people themselves. One could wish that the United Nations could stress this sort of message more. With all the love of beauty there is in the world it is still not too late.

Carved Chinese junk (replica of those used on Chinese rivers by well-to-do businessmen)
Writer's collection

Maurice Utrillo "Montmartre" (1935)
Writer's collection

Leon Gaspard "Frozen River with Walled-in Houses" (upper painting—1911)
Leon Gaspard "Russian Village" (lower painting—1911)
Pierre Auguste Renoir "Head of Gabrielle" (bronze sculpture—family edition of five)
Edvard Eriksen "The Little Mermaid" (bronze sculpture)
Chinse *sang de boeuf* porcelain lamp base
Writer's collection

Eugene Speicher
"The Caretaker's
Daughter" (1910)

Utamaro Two old p
Carved Chinese chai
Writer's collection

Jean Masson "Tahitian Children and Sea"
Writer's collection

Paul Jacoulet Four wood blocks
Chinese carved settee
17th century Hepplewhite Bookcase
Writer's collection

Martin-Ferrierés "Le Jardin de Crathes Castle" (about 1926)
Writer's collection

Pierre Auguste Renoir "Three Roses" (1890)
Writer's collection

AMERICA COMES OF AGE CULTURALLY

WHEN I was growing up, it was considered that one must finish one's education in Europe. No singer was deemed eligible who had not been trained abroad, and American art was not the in thing. But I was growing up in the early part of the century. As of today it appears that no country can claim exclusive precedence over all others. Talent and appreciation are widely disseminated. The covered wagons and the gold rush were phenomena of the 19th century. With the greater prosperity which the country generated after the Civil War people began to have more time for the development of the arts and sciences. Labor-saving devices and the generation of capital have created more leisure, and many, many people now have disposable time and money over which they can exercise some control.

Let us look at the development of art galleries. Surely the Metropolitan Museum in New York City is one of the great galleries of the world. Their Egyptian collection is one of the world's most special. Their permanent collection is outstanding. Most noteworthy is the management philosophy which keeps the institution constantly changing with alive new shows of great merit. Their show on 50 centuries of art which traced the development of arts and styles through 50 centuries with visual displays was a delight. Such endeavors develop an appreciation of art and also a unifying historical sense which are important in this day of questioning and insecure young people. Their period rooms also are an historical education. Even their gift shops which permit visitors to buy replicas at modest prices are worth noting. A cafeteria surrounding the classic pool makes it possible for people and families to enjoy the gallery in a leisurely way. It is a compliment to the Metropolitan to note the great throngs of visitors who are constantly in attendance. Surely it is true that the Metropolitan Museum has become a major factor in the life of New York City. So great a city as New York has many artistic centers. One of my favorite galleries is the Frick, with its gentle elegance and lovely Fragonards and exquisite antique furniture. The Whitney, Guggenheim and Modern Art museums also play integral roles in the life of the city, the latter three along more modern lines.

The major cities of the U.S.A. are all moving in this direction. Chicago has a great gallery. I have spent many hours there, in my stopovers between trains.

There are few lovelier spots in the country than the Legion of Honour in San Francisco—a replica of a French model—sitting on a windswept hill in sight of the Bay and the ocean and its charming cypress trees. The Legion of Honour recently had a reception in which it put on special display for the evening its finest French impressionist painting. It was a credit to San Francisco. Then there is the De Young Gallery in San Francisco, which houses the fabulous Avery Brundage collection of Oriental art, and which holds many great visiting shows such as the Rembrants, Van Goghs and others which go on the road every so often.

Los Angeles has come of age, and now has a gleaming white gallery set amidst fountains in the neighborhood of the old tar pits, and it is a credit to the enterprise of the City of Los Angeles.

Washington, D.C.'s magnificent National Gallery and Philadelphia's must also be added to any list. And coming to the smaller cities, Oakland, California, floated a bond issue and has completed an exceptionally attractive gallery, built in tiers on a hill, and is now in the business of collecting. It is devoting one floor to an historical collection of California and early day living; another to ecological displays, and one to an art collection. This gallery is a tremendous credit to Oakland.

My own small city of Sacramento has the Crocker Art Gallery and has just completed a new fireproof wing so that visiting exhibitions of distinction are willing to come here. A fine director is making the place sing with his original ideas. Special displays, one of tropical paintings, recently one for the blind, another of artifacts of California's wine industry, another of local collectors' acquisitions—all these keep interest alive and many people coming. Sunday afternoon concerts in the beautiful old ball room provide an outlet for many families and their children. The activities of the Crocker Art Gallery are sponsored by the Crocker Art Gallery Association, of which I have the privilege to be a life member. They organize public support for the various happenings at the Gallery, and I am sure ultimately will organize a drive to raise money for more exhibition space. Funds raised now by dues are used to purchase works of local artists of which Sacramento has quite a few, including the noted realist, Wayne Thiebaud, and my own special favorite, Gregory Kondos. The Gallery sponsors some excellent lecture programs and is the setting for the meetings of the Kingsley Club, a group of art-minded local ladies.

Symphony orchestras are developing all over the country. The New York Philharmonic, Philadelphia Orchestra, Boston Symphony, and Cleveland are among the greatest. Our own San Francisco has had an interesting development and has steadily advanced the quality and finesse of its productions to a truly great level. Again, my city of Sacramento has created a fine local symphony under the direction of Harry Newstone, an inspired conductor imported from London. It is the pride of the City that a Ford Foundation grant of $500,000 was matched by a local drive which came up with $500,000. For a city like Sacramento, this is no mean accomplishment. The whole city got in the act; large donors were tapped; auctions, dinner functions, reciprocal lunches all were arranged, and finally even $1.00 solicitations were sought to fill a large book of contributors. Finally the goal was reached. I serve on the Trust Foundation Board to help guard the principal; and it is a delight to participate in the spirit of dedication shared by businessmen, public spirited citizens, school children, housewives, musicians' unions, and the City Government to say nothing of the musicians themselves, to keep this project functioning. I am sure this sort of activity goes on all over the United States as an appreciation of art and music intensifies the zest for life and adds to its quality.

A burgeoning Little Theatre movement exists all over the country. From the true pros on Broadway to the traveling summer stock companies and the local amateur companies there is a great desire to experiment with the tried and known and also the unknown. Excellent Shakespearean companies exist. One of the greatest is at Ashland, Oregon, where fine direction and talent brought from all over the country combine to present an outstanding Shakespearean program for visitors from many states. This goes on every summer and has now for many years. There is Shakespeare on the Housatonic outside New York. The one time I went there I was delighted. The productions at Lincoln Center at the Vivian Beaumont Theatre are sometimes excellent, sometimes less so, but often fascinating. It is gratifying to see that a city like New York has been willing to spend such vast sums on its new opera house, Lincoln Center, and concert hall. Broadway often fascinates me, and the great stars are real personalities. Sometimes they are better than their vehicles, but a real star is still worth seeing. I suppose it may be that so much of Broadway theatre is aimed at expense account entertaining that it downgrades it sometimes, but it can still be very entertaining. I would say generally that Broadway theatre is still not as good as London. London has had the wit to keep its theatre more reasonable and tickets available, and the calibre of London theatre is very high indeed. But Broadway is still very entertaining even if it does leave something to be desired.

When companies go on tour, there is widespread interest. When the Bolshoi Ballet or the Royal Ballet or the Abbey Players take to the road, there is excellent response and the better productions are sold out weeks in advance. Such success surely bespeaks an avid national interest in good theatre and good musical productions.

Surely there is an interest in architecture, and beautiful new buildings throughout the country inspire widespread comment and discussions. Whether it is a beautiful skyscraper like the Seagram Building in New York or an unusual building like a Frank Lloyd Wright art gallery or a particularly interesting school, interest is high, and much experimentation is taking place.

I am fascinated by the market for excellent taste of one sort and another as demonstrated by the unique stores dealing in art which do make good money. I think of the host of small private galleries along 57th Street and upper Madison Avenue in New York City. Parke-Bernet and Sotheby are now merged so that the finest in artifacts are on sale in this country. Coming across the continent there is the excellent and highly regarded Maxwell Gallery in San Francisco which often has old masters of great merit and a director-owner of great perspicacity.

The evolution of Steuben Glass as an American art form is one that brings me special pleasure. It always seemed to me eminently suitable that President Eisenhower should give a Steuben piece to Queen Elizabeth of England as a wedding present, for it is truly American in its origin and development. The particular sparkle of Steuben Glass is unmatched. Their new series of limited editions and one-of-a-kind creations are giving the U.S.A. a magnificent art form, and they are now developing a host of outstanding artists and craftsmen who fashion their magnificent new masterpieces. James Houston and Pollard and Lloyd Atkins are among their greatest.

I treated myself once to one of their limited editions—an American eagle of 18-karat gold perched ready to soar into flight, on the edge of an exquisite glass crag, cut to resemble a great cliff. It is a masterpiece and catches the spirit of America's symbol, the eagle, in an inspiring way.

The fact that Steuben cannot get enough glass blowers to keep up with the demand speaks volumes for the acceptance of this beautiful art form by the American people.

More recently I have acquired another great piece— Magellan sailing through the straits into the Pacific, which he is about to name—a dramatic number in their limited edition historical series.

Style has come into the American home, and American families have found great pleasure in the creation of beautiful living quarters. A sophisticated association of interior decorators has developed, and it is a mark of achievement to be an A.I.D. Furnishing styles have developed along modern and traditional lines. At their best both developments are excellent. It has been my pleasure to know Mrs. Jean Carter, who has devoted a long and successful career to interior decorating. In addition to her exquisite taste she is warm enough to know that people should have some of their loved possessions about them, and she encourages her clients to keep and use old artifacts in which they have a personal interest or appeal. The fact that she has tailored a successful financial career out of her decorating speaks for her talent and the decorating interests of her many happy clients.

The number of home tours all over this country attests to the widespread interest in this subject. Whether it be the national displays at Natchez every year of beautiful old Southern homes or the many local home tours sponsored by opera guilds and the like, both reflect the interest in gracious living.

The country has developed a real passion for collection, whether stamps, antiques, first editions, medals or works of art. Any number of companies are now issuing annual editions of plates and platters. The very wealthy are putting together priceless collections of paintings gathered throughout the world.

In my own small way I have become a collector of sorts—not consciously at first, but just incidentally as I picked up objects I cherished on my trips. Then my love of beautiful painting led me to the purchase of a lovely Eugene Speicher child's portrait. I think of it as a child's Mona Lisa. I kept looking at it at Maxwell Galleries and admiring it so much I finally knew instinctively if I enjoyed it that much I should have it. There followed a Utrillo, for it seemed to bring to my own living room the mystique of Sacre Coeur which has long fascinated me. Then came a Renoir, he of the shining lights in his painting; and next two Gaspards, that talented Russian impressionist who has caught the spirit of pre-revolution Russian village life. There followed a Steuben piece, previously mentioned, and living artists whose work I admire—a Nong sculpture, three Gregory Kondos studies, a St. Francis by Bufano, Paul Jacoulet wood blocks, Ed Taylor wood blocks (he of Nevada City and Los Angeles). My latest acquisition was a charming painting of native children in Tahiti, painted by a French Tahitian painter, Jean Masson. I did not buy any of these treasures to sell. I have them all about me in my home, and they bring me daily joy and

Statue of St. Francis by Beniamino Bufano. Writer's collection.

peace, and I would hate to live without them. Beauty is its own excuse for being. They are a logical sequence, I suppose to my lifelong pleasure in art, first heightened by a course at Stanford devoted to great painting. Little did I think then that I would ever be able to have a Renoir and Utrillo of my own. It is another accomplishment of 20th Century development that income has been generated which has made possible a world of private art collecting by modest individuals as well as those of great wealth.

Then there is Metropolitan Opera in New York—not to mention San Francisco which has its own season every fall. The Opera Guild of Sacramento knocks itself out to bring an evening of grand opera once a year to Sacramento— an evening of elegance which helps to elevate taste in a period when many are trying to reduce everyone to the lowest common denominator. A number of us underwrite the annual opera appearance as it does not carry itself financially.

My sister and her husband have been identified for many years with the Community Church in New York City. My brother-in-law, Arthur Frantz, is the music director of this well known church, and the organ music and exquisite choir renditions are a real privilege to hear. I attend whenever I have a Sunday in New York City. It is like going to a small symphony concert.

One of my more pleasant recent experiences was having my portrait painted by Felix de Cossio of New York City. He and his wife are both highly talented artists, Cuban refugees who lost heavily in the revolution. They came to this country, became American citizens, established their studio overlooking Gramercy Park, and have developed a very successful professional life for themselves, and both do exquisite work. What fun it was to sit for the painting, with that dear Mrs. de Cossio talking to me of their life in Cuba and this country while her husband painted. Then lunch would be brought in—always with some muscatel wine—and we relaxed and exchanged further pleasantries.

Certainly my life has been made richer by my being able to taste of the delights of the world of culture, art, and music. My enjoyment has of course always been as an amateur observer—for my workaday hours have been those of a business woman—in Sacramento, Montgomery Street and Wall Street. An appreciation of beauty heightens the senses and sharpens one's perception of business, political, and personal processes. It improves the qualities of life. We must count as one of the blessings of 20th Century living the opportunities which have been afforded us of participating in the joys of an advancing culture.

Gregory Kondos "Streets of Mykonos" (1970)
Writer's collection

Gregory Kondos "Eldorado Oaks" (1969)
Writer's collection

Steuben Eagle Rock, Designed by James Houston, in Writer's Collection.

Steuben Ferdinand Magellan, Designed by Lloyd Atkins, in Writer's Collection.

EVOLUTION OF SECURITY ANALYSIS

RUNNING parallel to the years which this account covers was the development of the whole process of security analysis. Since this evolution reflected the growth of more sophisticated business procedures as well as a heightened sense of the moral proprieties of proper investment practices, the subject holds some historic interest.

Prior to the Depression of the 30's, investment work tended to be done in a rather haphazard way. Branch banking had not yet established itself, and locally owned banks were inclined to have a senior officer pick up securities on the basis of brokers' stories. Naturally some officers were better than others. Insurance companies likewise had nothing resembling the present investment departments, and research and development were waiting in the wings. The S.E.C. did not exist in its present form. The financial debacle of the 30's changed all this. The magnitude of the defaults and the bankruptcies which were then precipitated increased the general awareness that new procedures were indicated.

Excellent writers like Graham and Dodd emerged on the scene with textbooks describing the process of ratio analysis and the scientific study of management. The more astute banks like the old Wells Fargo and Bankers Trust pioneered in the creation of analytical departments; and impartial rational studies were made of all the investments in which they were interested. At the same time considerable thought was given to the need for intellectual honesty in analyzing securities in companies which might happen to be clients of the banks in question. To the everlasting credit of the pioneers in this work, close adherence was given to avoiding conflicts of interest. One large central bank after another started building analytical departments. As local banks more and more sold out to the great banking chains, it soon developed that analytical work tended to be concentrated in the big city headquarters, or in the case of trust companies and later mutual funds in certain centers like Boston. Local financial concerns developed some sort of correspondent or counseling connection with big city headquarters. An advisory relationship thus tended to develop with the result that analytical departments were called on more and more often and the size of the departments increased very materially.

At the beginning the requirements and qualifications of an analyst were rather nebulous. As leaders in this development emerged they tended to train young people who showed an aptitude and who appeared to have the qualities of scholarship and judgment which were needed.

Then came the creation of the Security Analyst societies, as the need was felt for the exchange of information and the creation of some standards. This development was accelerating after World War II because the market which had been on the bargain counter in 1948 was showing real recovery in the decade of the 50's. Investors began to return to the market in increasing numbers and wanted more and more advice as they did not wish to repeat the mistakes of the Depression. Security Analyst societies multiplied and from original beginnings in such cities as Chicago, New York, Boston, and San Francisco, they were soon being chartered in every area of the country. There was discussion as to admission requirements, but generally it was not too hard to gain membership. An applicant who had a specified minimum period of service in the business either with an institution or counseling firm was usually accepted for membership.

In the earlier days of Financial Analyst societies they tended to be more selective than they are now in that members were likely to know the new applicants. Inevitably as they grew larger they developed both strengths and weaknesses. A strength was greater financial assets which enabled them to be run in a businesslike way—with money available to engage dining rooms on a regular basis, send out proper notices, and arrange for good speakers. As the societies became more and more important, major firms wished to make appearances before the analysts' groups. The membership of the societies was in control of astronomical amounts of money, and companies who wanted to do financing cared about keeping in well with the F.A.F.* membership. At the annual meeting national speakers of note participated, and Federal Reserve officials would come to discuss their current philosophy. Leading firms like Salomon Brothers sent their best speakers on interest rates and credit. Field trips offered expeditions to American Telephone laboratories, General Motors proving grounds, Philadelphia industrial developments, and the NASA headquarters at Houston, among others.

Inevitably as the meetings became more prestigious attendance increased, so that national meetings became very congested. Promoters started coming, and operators came to entertain the analysts, and the younger or less professional of the membership sometimes succumbed to the growing commercialism and politicking. The original rare intellectual atmosphere began to get a little smoggy.

I remember being shocked at a luncheon one day when a young promoter at my table was expounding on how to squeeze more out of his client. I interposed a comment that these tactics did not consider the client's welfare very much, and he replied that I paid too much attention to the client.

The very success of the early analysts' groups and the prestige they attained were instrumental in attracting some of the wrong people, and thus even further developments were brought about.

The C.F.A. was the next step. C.F.A. stands for Chartered Financial Analyst, and the creation of this Association was an attempt to establish a professional status to the business of security analysis. From the very beginning the movement met with approbation. The program consists of three examinations; the first covering some of the basic fundamentals of analysis, the second accounting and analytical procedures, and the third the wide range of portfolio management principles together with discussions of the ethics of finance in its larger ramifications.

On first thought I was not enthusiastic about trying for the C.F.A. Charter, knowing it would involve considerable

*Financial Analysts Federation

preparation and I was already extremely busy, as I was by this time running our sizable portfolio. Furthermore, I had already established something of a professional reputation, and the possibility of failure would inevitably jeopardize that recognition.

One day I discussed this with Herbert Drake, a senior vice-president of Crocker Bank, and he was unequivocal in saying that it was my duty to take it. Since he was a man whose brilliance and integrity I had long admired, I naturally attached considerable weight to this position. He emphasized that it was only by the leaders in the business supporting this new venture that the proper importance could be allocated to it; and that if we did not give it our moral support, it might never get off the ground. His point was well taken, as we all recognized the need to try to build the professional aspects and weed out the promotional shades of the business.

As I started my preparations this became more apparent. The meticulous quality even of allowing an applicant to stand for the examinations was something. Birth certificates and citizenship papers had to be certified; a photostat copy was not enough. Every effort was made to exclude international charlatans. The philosophical nature of the ethical questions raised were those only a mature analyst could grasp. As a result, I would say that while the C.F.A. Charter surely does not guarantee that the holder is necessarily going to make the most money, it does carry a reasonable confidence that the investor is dealing with a person of high ethical and scholarly attainments who does understand the true nature of the responsibilities involved.

From the inception the program met with success. Study groups were organized in larger areas so applicants could train together. Seminars are now being sponsored to aid in preparation for the examinations. This is all to the good.

I studied before it had become so established, and worked at night and wrote out trial runs of possible questions. I exchanged papers with Charlie Minard of the San Francisco Society, an analyst I had known as far back as Stanford University days. Exchange of ideas is helpful and fortunately we both passed. I went down to Los Angeles for the examination, for I experienced considerable trepidation, and wanted to take it where I did not know so many people and did not want to get into a lot of conversations to distract me. It truly was not hard to return to the processes of a student; what was difficult was the number of interruptions; for a person in business has the never ending task of planning his own programs for his office, and much of this is inevitably done away from one's desk.

Providence smiled upon me, and I became a C.F.A. The Charter has brought me pride and satisfaction, and status does go with it. The Charter means that the holder has been exposed to a good deal of the best in the business and does have some sophistication. Institutions now show with some pride how many of the analytical staff members are C.F.A.'s and some smaller advisory firms will not allow anyone to become a fully fledged staff member who is not a C.F.A.

It is a justifiable conclusion, I believe, to say that the C.F.A. movement has established itself and has gone a long way toward bringing a professional quality to this activity. Whereas it was originally hoped that after ten years there might be 300 C.F.A.'s, there are already around 3,000.

There is a place for both the larger organization of the Financial Analysts and the C.F.A., which is the brainchild of the larger organization and operates under its auspices and with its blessings. The C.A.F. can plan the large meetings and has the size to attract important speakers; it runs the *Financial Analysts' Magazine*, which is the trade journal of the business and has many current articles of interest. I have been honored by having several articles published therein. It has the staff to plan national conventions and initiate seminars, and is run on an inclusive rather than exclusive basis. At its best, it can be very good, and some of its programs are of very high calibre. Others, such as a seminar on the social responsibilities of business which I attended, provided a platform for at least some ambitious young speakers who in my humble opinion were more interested in providing publicity for themselves than they were in furthering knowledge. This kind of development has in turn led to a new ramification.

There are now many more private invitational luncheon meetings than there used to be. Some of the S.E.C. requirements about full disclosure have made corporation officials more cautious of public appearances as they are not certain when they may be violating an S.E.C. rule. The press is generally not invited to the private luncheons, and speakers are more relaxed about expressing opinions. They are very careful not to reveal any information which is not public, but they are more inclined to voice their own thinking. These private lunches are sponsored sometimes by investment houses and sometimes by corporations who wish to meet with their larger institutional stockholders.

The private lunches do tend to draw people away from the analysts' meetings, but surely there is a place for both of them.

Private seminars of note are sponsored by leading firms. A quite famous annual affair is the invitational seminar sponsored by Sutro and Co. in Los Angeles every spring. It is known affectionately as Felix's Bash. It is such a beautifully planned affair with fine programs and excellent hospitality provided that somehow it became an event everyone wanted to attend. Analysts soon learned that four days at the Sutro Seminar were the equivalent of a week on Wall Street for the major financial institutions send representatives and there is an interchange of information. Sharing breakfast, lunch and dinner together with leading corporate officers provides an outstanding access to interesting information and personalities. The charm of the whole Sutro group welcomes all the guests. Expeditions to the *Queen Mary* at Long Beach, the Irvine properties out of Los Angeles, the Lion Safari intersperse a little lightness and fun into a very concentrated program. And the dinner dance at the Felix Juda's beautiful home with little bunches of white gardenias hanging from the great tent which covers the garden for the evening—plus the wonderful friendliness of the entire Juda family—is it any wonder that guests come from far and near for this event?

Another phase of the development of investment analysis which should be mentioned is performance investing, and its newest facet, the concept of measuring risk. In an earlier part of this paper reference was made to the measurement of performance and its fallacies. The writer once had an article published in the *Financial Analysts Journal* (subsequently read into the *Congressional Record*) on this subject, so her disapproval of the performance syndrome is a matter of record. The performance racket was an immature effort at best to discredit responsible trust companies and advisors for seemingly lackluster performances while at the same time building up the so-called young stars who had meteorlike careers in the 1968 market and who collapsed in 1969 and 1970 with results which wiped out many people who never will recover their losses. The whole movement was a reprehensible one and pushed some solid institutions into short term speculations and away from the accepted principles of long term investing.

Fortunately the more innovative in the business have now come up with a new effort at measuring risk and relating it to performance. This makes much more sense, as it enables an investor to make some sort of determination as to how much risk he can afford to take. The type of investment which soars 60% in a short period is just as likely to lose 75% in an equally short period and in fact may be wiped out. Various new formplae are now being experimented with which involve assigning a *beta* or risk factor to individual securities, based on their volatility in transactions of millions of shares. High-powered computers make this measurement possible. The higher the risk the higher the *beta* and .60 or .70 fairly low. On the basis of the *beta* factor, stocks can then be classified into deciles from 1 to 10, and low risk stocks, like utilities, major oils, and banks tend to be in the low deciles while airlines and other high risk stocks tend to be in the high deciles. Admittedly this is new territory and the measurements are hypothetical and probably many subsequent modifications will be made. The *beta* factors are coordinated with some guide like the Standard & Poor's 500 or other yardstick. Allowing for the fact that any new development should be used with discretion and judgment, it now becomes possible to classify accounts as aggressive, average, income or other level and to define one's goals. A manager can say which are the objectives of an account, and an investor can choose his account or fund or individual investment after defining his own objectives. School teachers can identify a fund suitable to their own capacity for taking risks and businessmen can choose the funds which are more compatible for them.

Since there is yet no way to read the future and unexpected developments may always occur in the way of new incentives, obsolescence and changing management capabilities, any such formula must be used with judgment. It can be a very valuable adjunct to good business decisions when used with moderation. The tendency in some quarters to measure results down to a gnat's eyelash is ill-advised and over use of a guide can lead to its rejection. Properly used the identification of risk is a very progressive forward step.

No remarks on the evolution of financial analysis would be complete without mention of the S.E.C. This powerful organization was created to regulate market activities after the self destructive period culminating in 1929. As mutual funds became more sizeable in the long recovery period developing after World War II the S.E.C. became ever more active in trying to eliminate abuses and keep promoters within bounds. Its activities have been directed toward protecting the investor and curbing abuses. While there had to be much trial and error in an emerging field, their overall record has been highly commendable. Their goals in effect were the same as the C.F.A. although approached from a different angle; namely, to heighten financial responsibility and moral propriety. These are not easy goals, to be sure, but they are essential in a civilized business climate. In spite of the controversies which have surrounded the S.E.C., rare is the businessman who would want to see it eliminated. It is a necessary and valuable part of the business community, and has made a real contribution. Financial analysts and the S.E.C. have learned to live together, and this is a relationship which is going to continue.

The whole subject of financial analysis has been related to the growth of capital in this country. The great need for it became apparent as the public awoke to the fortunes that had been made in the 50's through investment. By the time the public had become aware of the bonanza, we were in the 60's, the market was no longer on the bargain counter, and indeed by the late 60's, bonds were proving more rewarding than stocks. Where the 70's will lead us only time will tell.

Under the duress of the emotional surge which is directed toward rearranging social priorities, while at the same time virtually ignoring the need to produce in order to have the goods to distribute, we could move into a period of sharing the poverty instead of sharing the wealth. If the generation of capital is slowed down or almost halted, the ones who do have any capital will have an asset even more precious than it now appears. It could therefore develop that in preparation for such a period, the accumulation of a certain portion of one's assets in cash and liquid assets might be the smartest near term move.

For in such a period the wages of capital might be higher than they now are. All of which is to say that the future of financial analysis cannot be divorced from the political and social outlook.

Once a man in my office was asking for some financial advice. I couched my answer in terms of this same political and social outlook. My questioner was horrified, and exclaimed: "Miss Ritter, you're talking politics!"

Good financial analysis cannot do otherwise.

WOMEN IN BUSINESS

ONE EXTREME creates another. If Women's Lib amazes, confounds and antagonizes many people, it must be remembered that it is a sequel to many years of injustice to working women.

The solid part of the Women's Rights Movement has come from very real problems. The Women's Rights Movement is often incorrectly interpreted to be an anti-man, anti-family, anti-children development. As such it has been belittled and maligned and laughed at by people who should know better. The pretty wife of a well known state governor recently took it upon herself to announce that woman's place is in the home. A woman of inherited money whose husband is a big earner—what does she know of the mother whose husband is dead and has children to support and no money? Is she saying that this woman should go on relief and that her children should be satisfied with handouts? If this needy woman wishes to work and does not receive equal pay for equal work, she is being condemned to exploitation. Is this the alternative the governor's pretty wife suggests? Most women work for the same reason most men work—they need the money.

There are any number of reasons why women need to work. We no longer live in an agrarian society where families have an extra bedroom for unmarried females in the family. Daughters have to get out and get on their own as much as sons. For every man who does not marry, for every man who goes to war, for every man who divorces, lands in prison, suffers serious illness or other mishaps, there is a woman who has to provide her own sustenance, or a good part thereof. It is inevitable therefore that present-day social conditions require many women to work, and this they are doing in increasing numbers. Inflation has aggravated the situation. A growing number of families of modest means need a second income, and this can be said of some of better than modest means.

It was a natural sequence, therefore, with the growing number of working women, that a revolt should have developed among them in an effort to eliminate exploitation and win greater economic rewards. Truly, I am surprised that the movement has been so long coming. The increased volume of voices is winning a response which smaller earlier groups were never able to elicit.

The sounder part of the movement is asking only for fair play and not for special privileges. Women are not asking to be favored with positions they have not been trained to handle; they *are* asking for equal pay for equal work, and they are asking for proper consideration when they apply for better jobs. Women should not be condemned always to the poorest quality jobs when the men get the promotions and the special rewards. From time immemorial personnel departments of big companies have shuffled the applications so much that there rarely seemed to be a good job available when a woman was applying.

Women are tired of this type of subordination. It has been surprising, actually, that other minority complaints were listened to more readily than women's. Our society began a process of selection by quota along racial and ethnic lines long before it paid attention to women's rights. Colleges adjusted their admission procedures to conform to racial representations. Business organizations, sometimes of their own volition, and sometimes under pressure from government, started modifying their hiring practices to parallel the composition of their communities. Civil rights marches were organized along racial or economic lines, and church groups became quite activist in supporting these demonstrations either openly or surreptitiously. The theatre was full of racial overtones and rock music grew out of much primitive African background. During this period violence grew and riots participated in by racial antagonists did millions of dollars worth of damage. As a working woman I was disappointed that society as a whole, while paying a great deal of attention to noisy activist minority groups, seemed unaware or blind to the inferior economic position of the working woman.

Finally many women, who had no other recourse open to them, became very troublesome too.

Human nature being what it is, reform movements tend to take both the high road and the low road. I have long felt that one way individual women could advance themselves was to develop special talents, and be very good in particular fields. Merchandising was an area where women could become very successful as buyers. Design and high fashion have produced the likes of Coco Chanel, Adele Simpson, Pauline Trigere, Mary Quant, Jeanne Lanvin, Matthews. Newspaper reporting and publishing have come up with Mary McGrory, Dorothy Schiff, Eleanor McClatchy of the *Sacramento Bee*, Mae Belle Pendergast of the *Sacramento Union*, Clare Booth Luce. In politics we have Margaret Chase Smith, Yvonne Braithwaite Burke, Shirley Chisholm, Bella Abzug, and others. In finance if a woman makes money for an account she manages, people could not care less about her sex, and they will continue to engage a winner. The large Los Angeles Retirement Fund is supervised by my friend, Janet Codding. Firemen's Fund has a woman vice-president in securities, and my own company has favored me for these many years. Sylvia Porter is brilliant as a financial writer.

Interior decorating has used the talents of many artistic women. And in sciences, the medical profession and research, women have often distinguished themselves. However, it must be recognized that the above mentioned are the particularly fortunate, and necessarily there are many women who do not have a special talent to develop or who came to earning their living late enough in life that they find it difficult to develop a specialty.

There was once a very successful Negro salesman in our company. He died of a ruptured appendix. I often remember his opinion that minorities must not expect special privileges or particular breaks. They do want to be able to compete openly and fairly. Extending special privileges to incapable people places a great burden upon the productive system and is ultimately costly to everyone. The same goes for women. They should not be promoted merely because someone feels sorry for them, or the company can point with pride and say, "Look, we promoted Miss So and So."

I can agree with men executives who say they do not want to promote women just because they are women. Most women are not asking for that. Contrarily, what has happened millions of times is that women are denied promotions just because they are women. Businessmen should concern themselves about this. Countless times women have carried the real responsibilities and done the real work, and found themselves carrying only partially competent young men who subsequently received the promotions and better raises. If women are not exposed to real responsibilities and clued in on what is going on in a firm, it is not possible then for them to be able to compete with a man who is in line for promotion when the opportunity comes.

This is the area of the terrible discrimination against women. No honest person can deny that this discrimination exists. Shirley Chisholm said she had encountered more discrimination because of being a woman than because of being a black. In my own case I know that my advancement came much more slowly than it would have had I been a man. The reason that I live as well as I do today is that I made money in the market, which treats a woman's dollar the same as a man's.

The terrible irony of all this is that society, in failing to use its talents where it finds them, is retarding its own progress.

This situation which I have been discussing became more and more aggravated as more women worked. The increase in the number of working women accelerated during the Depression and subsequent wars, so that there is now a much larger working force than heretofore which considers itself abused and mistreated.

During the Depression and war years, there was hardly time for a movement to develop. John Kennedy took an early initiative in this area by creating an Advisory Commission on the Status of Women. This went over so well that similar commissions were created in many states. These commissions directed their work to various areas, including improved educational opportunities, revised legal protection for women in exercising rights to their own property, improved pay standards in labor negotiations, child care centers for working mothers, and similar matters. In our own Democratic Women's Club we created a committee of which I served as chairman, whose objective was to study the reports of the advisory commissions on the status of women and then implement and support the recommendations as they came along in the best manner possible. Unfortunately during administrations subsequent to Governor Pat Brown's, the budget was cut for the California Commission, and the research was reduced to a much more limited status. I have attended some of the recent meetings in Sacramento and get the impression that their program needs to be a little more clearly spelled out. It appears the present administration does not give it much support.

In the meantime Women's Lib has arrived as the big attention getter in the movement and has provided the listening world with a considerable amount of sound and fury. Some of it is constructive; some of it less so.

In its many facets the Women's Rights Crusade is moving along, and many previously locked doors are opened to both sexes. Public opinion is becoming so strong on this subject that companies are increasingly afraid to defy it, and we are seeing a constantly heightening flow of able women into executive positions and the policy making level. An Equal Rights Amendment is being considered. Some states have already ratified it—others are delaying—and my own state has bottled it up because the committee chairman said he could not bring himself to approve a bill that could send his small daughters off to war. But some day it will make it.

This whole performance has been close to my heart because I could not be otherwise than deeply committed to its success. Earning one's livelihood in a highly competitive society is difficult at best; to have the additional burden of sex discrimination has made the lives of many working women a hopeless tedium.

It is my own personal philosophy that one must make one's life a series of opportunities rather than a series of stumbling blocks. We live in an ebullient society that is demonstrating its tolerance of all sorts of burgeoning movements. So women do not need to be discouraged; and neither do the executives who despair of what they consider the whole sorry business.

There is plenty of opportunity for the woman of intelligence, dignity, and honor. If she can do her assignment in an efficient and candid way, recognition almost surely lies ahead. The opportunities are abundantly greater today for a woman earner than they were near the turn of the century.

I am writing this part of my narrative on the giant ocean liner *France* on a passage to Paris for a little holiday. I am charmed with the women I have been meeting on this ship. At my table there is a well known political writer (a warm hearted lovely person), who is traveling with her precious dog; there is a spry little travel agent who has five telephones on her desk. A Red Cross social worker is another nice human being in the group.

There are plenty of happy women who have lived a full life working; a woman with an optimistic forward-looking frame of mind can do wonders for herself. Bitterness destroys the soul, and working women who succumb to bitterness poison their own happiness. Rather, if the working sisters try to make this the best of all possible worlds, they can be thankful for the newly found advantages which have been won for them; they can give a salute to Woman's Lib, support other women when they can, and do everything possible in the way of self-improvement to better their own chances for advancement. They can also check on which legislators and politicians are articulate in support of equal rights.

There are many decent men in the business world. The men of true stature are willing to recognize ability wherever it exists. Men at the management level are often very broad in their attitude toward the whole problem. When I remember some of the great businessmen like Peter Cook and Arthur Luddy and George Pollock and George Gibson and Jo Bickford and Charles LeRoy at Eastman Dillon, and Gerald Hahn and Virgil O'Sullivan, I am reminded that we women have been aided in our long crusade by men of broad perspective. Middle-class fathers of bright daughters tend to be interested in this situation. With the help also of the Shirley Chisholms, Margaret Chase Smiths, Martha Griffiths and the like, we have much working in our favor. Let us support the broader aspects of the Equal Rights Movement and be proud to do it. The day has passed to suffer ridicule

127

lightly. We can find our own ways to wither those who give only lip service to the problem.

I attended a fascinating invitational symposium recently sponsored by the Bank of America and *The Ladies Home Journal* on Women in the Economy. I was most encouraged to see the number of brilliant women there giving rigorous support to improving the status of working women. Participating were Sylvia Porter, Liz Carpenter, Claire Giannini Hoffman, Lynda Johnson Robb, Myrlie Evers, Esther Peterson, Martha Griffiths and other brilliant and successful women.

And so, my working sisters, with grace in your step, a song in your heart, self-discipline to make the most of yourself and improve your own potential, you can go a long way. Let us appreciate those who have helped us get this far, and by precept and example let us lead the way forward.

VIGNETTES

LIFE IS warm and fun, and with all the political and business and social and cultural problems there is still time for some sparkle and zest. All the charming little human exchanges can make a wonderful world department.

* * *

Here I am in Paris again. The boat train came in from the ship through the lovely French farm lands, past Rouen, neat factories, successful-looking power developments. Suddenly there was the Eiffel Tower beside us. The family sitting in front of me started gathering its packages. One knew from their conversation they had not been to Paris before, but the father said they had arrived. The puzzled worried small boy said, "But Dad, how do you *know* this is Paris?" Some day the Eiffel Tower will be a landmark to him also.

* * *

Today my niece brought her two little sons, five and six, to have lunch with me in the Ritz garden. The children are bilingual, having a French father and American mother, and having divided their short lives among Holland, U.S.A. and France. The younger one was quite worried for fear he would not be able to converse fluently with his Aunt Lucy from America, as he thought he might have forgotten some of his English. He need not have worried. His greeting kiss would have been understood in any language. The older one immediately wanted to know how they turned the fountain on, and inspected all the flowers in the Ritz garden, seeking a switch. He was only moderately satisfied when the waiter explained they were controlled by a pump down under the ground. Everyone in the garden dining room smiled at the conversation and the beautiful children. Upstairs they inspected the light fixtures and plumbing, and gave a rundown on all the features, to their father at dinner that night.

* * *

The Chanel fashion show this afternoon was one facet of French talent at its supreme best. Lithe beautiful girls with reed-like bodies came in with their quick little steps, modeling the famous understated Chanel suits, as only that illustrious house can do them. Each girl held up the number of the outfit she was showing as she turned and stepped, whirling the supple skirts. Materials breathtakingly beautiful, flawless tailoring, surprising uses of fur as lining for coats, and one with a white mink panel down the front—all these were shown in quick succession as one after another stunning creation was presented. Suits were handsomely woven wools with bright metallic blouses making them surprisingly dressy. And then there were the little black numbers. And no one could beat Chanel at that. Evening dresses of metallic brocades brought the afternoon to a close. The famous staircase where Chanel used to sit was in the background. Quite a group of Oriental ladies was present, and they were generous in their applause. Two lovely American girls from Sacramento accompanied me. At the close we all knew we had seen something very special.

* * *

Twice today a sob almost welled up within me; first at the Louvre when I stood beside the Winged Victory of Samothrace, done around 200 B.C., and preserved by those who appreciate beauty all these years. Think of the imagination of that early sculptor doing those great magnificent wings, with his painstaking workmanship. And later in the day the organ music was rolling and reverberating through the great arches of Notre Dame, overwhelming the listener with its spirit and grandeur. The church was filled with young people with knapsacks on their backs, their faces uplifted, watching the deep colors of the rose windows while the music pealed and rolled in waves overhead. These young people were there because they wanted to be—not because they had to be. Paris must be one of the most civilized places in the whole world.

* * *

The day before I had been visiting with a young French broker in his office with a view of Sacré Coeur out the window. We touched on the war in Vietnam and its uselessness; he mentioned that he had fought in Algeria, and thinks still of the good friends of his who were killed—for what purpose? He said the people in Vietnam would be better off if the world would leave them alone. And years later we are still at it, though the war is grinding down. The Frenchman raised the question whether the futility of the Vietnam situation might not be teaching its lesson that war is a foolish instrument of national policy and accomplishes nothing. Might politicians really learn from their failure here how disliked war is and abandon it as a weapon?

* * *

My niece Nancy and I flew into Berlin as a little extra dividend. The graceful French Caravelle deposited us seemingly effortlessly with a minimum of fanfare, and soon we were ensconced at the Hotel Kempinski, which has the dubious distinction of being Hitler's old headquarters. West Berlin is sparkling and energetic. They have erected a modern new church beside the shattered Kaiser Wilhelm Memorial, which has been retained as a reminder of what happened to them. One looks at the faces of these determined-looking people and respects their pluck in rebuilding their damaged city and starting up anew. There are new hotels, colorful restaurants, tall clean buildings, an Olympic stadium, bustling stores exhibiting the finest in German leather work, clocks beyond number, and Rosenthal and Meissen china. Cars and buses are everywhere with a liberal sprinkling of hippies. But it is unnatural. For there through the middle of the city is that atrocious wall. On the East Berlin side there are numerous block houses with guards and telescopes trained on all activity. East Berlin must have an enormous electric bill to pay for all the searchlights illuminating the wall. On the East Berlin side there are no flowers; the lawns are badly kept; there are few cars around and fewer people. Where are they all? East Berlin won most of the fine old buildings when the division was made, including the University, museum, theatres and most of the royal palaces. One wonders what they teach in the University now. Tourist buses are allowed into East Berlin at present, and we took one. They drive into a sort of no-man's land; everyone gets out for passport inspection; an East German guide takes over, and the tour starts past the gray grim looking city. The guide's talk is full of childlike propaganda, but of course he cannot help himself. He has to do what he is told. The stores are stocked with goods as plain as what one finds in Russian cities. There are some tall new buildings, prefabricated according to the guide, so obviously some money is being spent. The marked contrast on the two sides of the wall makes one feel really very sad. Supposedly many people on both sides of the wall are tied to it because their homes and loved ones are there. Where will it all end? Having just come from the beauty of civilized Paris, the stark grimness of East Berlin stands out in great contrast. Even in West Berlin, in spite of the determined good spirits, what can the people do? They are surrounded by enemy territory and cannot venture but a few miles out from the heart of town. The wall is a patchwork of stucco plaster, barbed wire and vacant buildings with broken windows. When we had driven around the area, we drove back to no-man's land, all alighted and went through passport inspection again, and returned to lively West Berlin, and an elegant dinner out in the lush garden terrace of the Berlin Hilton. With a heavy heart one knew that this kind of existence would break the real heart of a city, in spite of all its pluck and courage.

We returned to Paris on the Caravelle and had a pleasant flight, replete with champagne, *petit fours* and other French delicacies. We did not know then that an East Berlin plane had exploded that morning on takeoff, killing 156 people. We landed at Orly after an hour and 45 minutes flight, and were greeted by two beautiful little French boys. How lucky can we be? West Berlin is brave, but Paris is happy.

And this afternoon we went to the Givenchy fashion show—truly fabulous. The imagination and flare of the many presentations were surely appreciated by the engrossed audience, who knew that they were viewing the creations of a master. From the shiny plastic materials of the ski outfits to the exquisite sequined gowns and furred and feathered ensembles, it was a show to make one catch one's breath. Paris, you just go on and on with more surprises. It makes you what you are—beautiful, talented, very busy, traffic frenetic, and an inordinate amount of common sense that stirs the whole mixture into an enchanting potpourri. (And I'll let you in on a little secret. The bankers have told me this week that the French economy is leading the world just now and people from other nations are pouring money into France for investment purposes—so much in fact that the Bank of France is keeping a wary eye on the situation so that too much outside money does not come in and take over the country. Heaven forbid! Don't let France become less French.)

* * *

Now I am in a beautiful park next to Versailles. There are velvety green fields outside my balcony and bleating sheep to add to the pastoral scene. A tour through the magnificent old Palace of Versailles this morning reminds one of the lessons of history. Where are they now—the royal line and their artists who created all that beauty? Tumbled from power at a cost of their heads because they did not learn in time that life demands moderation, a balancing of power between the rich and the humble, an ebb and flow between beauty and the plain, the brilliant and the simple.

I think of some of our problems at home; that the State of California says it will close San Quentin Prison because, among other reasons, there is too much violence there and it destroys human beings. Is it San Quentin that destroys them or were they broken before they reached there—sometimes because they are the dropouts which any society tosses aside and only sometimes because society is at fault. I have had more than passing interest in this situation since my very decent brother, Irving, is business manager of that once mammoth institution. Indeed, friends have said they were comforted to know that such a man as Irving Ritter was among those in the top echelon there, because it insured that there was an element of fairplay and intelligent discipline. The newspapers whip up public opinion among the activists, but is society to succumb to all the people who try to smuggle guns into the prisons? Does not some fault lie with them? Are not the hardworking straight people entitled to some protection? While a world of sympathy develops for gangsters, dopesters and freaks, the quiet people who work and pay taxes are often treated with impatience and given short shrift. Will we solve our problems more wisely than the rabble of the French revolution?

Recently I had the unfortunate experience of being knocked down from behind, without warning, by a 21-year-old girl who tried to steal my purse. Fortunately she was apprehended as my screams brought me a rescuer in the person of a responsible businessman. The girl confessed but was released on bail. Will she try again on some other victim?

I have a fine young nephew, Michael Ritter, who has gone into police work and is very dedicated about it. It is without question one of the hardest, most dangerous and most underpaid of ways to earn a living—also one of the most vital and essential to a responsible society. Public opinion needs to give more backing to the sturdy people like our police and less to the Black Panthers and radical chic who stir up the troublemakers. Astute magazines recently have been emphasizing the need for mobilizing support for our young policemen, salary-wise, and giving them the moral backing and position in the community to which they are entitled.

I say amen to that. I think of my nephew's beautiful wife and children and the risks they all carry for society. His exquisite little daughter looks like Alice in Wonderland and the small boy has a smile that befriends his world.

One of the reasons the Democratic Party has been slipping lately is that it has catered to too many odd characters and has been strangely silent in its support of responsible hardworking people who carry the burdens. It needs to return to the combination of the true liberality and common sense which built it in the first place. A true liberal is a very different person from a radical, who tends to exercise a form of tyranny.

* * *

Enjoying the great liner *The France* brings to mind American shipping. There are now only two American passenger ships left on the high seas, and these may not last long. Our labor policies have rendered our merchant ships uncompetitive. My excellent brother, Ovid Ritter, has been in shipping all his life until his recent retirement. Hence I have heard many discussions of this. Time after time, long protracted strikes promoted by unions have trimmed the profits so extensively that American capital will no longer go into this field. We have abdicated to the rest of the world. And who was willing to listen during the gradual strangling of the industry?

Presumably we will not have a revolution as some activists wish, because public opinion is beginning to crystallize back to the middle of the road. The country is essentially too sound for a revolution. Being in France makes one aware that downfalls of the likes of Versailles and the Bastille can be avoided. The American political system is lumbering its slow way toward an accommodation with common sense. The Democrats took it away from the Republicans when the latter collapsed in the Depression due to a combination of failures (including blindness). The Republicans are now taking it away from the Democrats, because the Democrats have let the farout fringe win too much control, and that is not acceptable to the mainstream of American thinking. The ebb and the flow, the *yin* and the *yang*, save us all in time.

* * *

I have a personable sparkling niece named Lucianne who lives in Palo Alto with her husband and three dear young children. A visit to them is a time of joy. The ten-year-old brother picks up his infant sister and carries her around like the responsible little man he is. When I cannot understand

135

what the baby sister is saying, the little brother supplies his interpretation and says she is telling you so and so. This family has worked hard improving its home, laying bricks in the court yard, planting colorful flowers that provide a myriad of lovely tones, and feeding the family dog and hamster. Recently a mob of rioting students from nearby Stanford University went past their house to an objective further away on Page Mill Road, where the electronics plants are. The residents had their taste of fear and apprehension as the noisy jostling demonstrators overflowed on the front yards as they went by. How easily an incident could turn into tragedy. And who can control a mob?

Such a thing would never have happened when I was at Stanford. Is this progress? So much money was spent repairing broken windows and other damage at Stanford last year (reportedly $250,000) that this year the broken windows are just left, either boarded up or covered with paper strips. It is most likely that some of the trouble makers at Stanford come from off campus, but whoever they are, they are undisciplined young, bent on trouble. They make it harder for Stanford to attain its maximum.

* * *

Every generation has different burdens. My generation had the two world wars and Depression. Today's generation has Vietnam (a less justifiable and more frustrating situation, although not so devastating), inflation, drugs, and racial tensions, plus an ecology awareness. It also has the pill, which for the first time in history effectively separates procreation from sex life. In addition it has more money and lives better than any previous generation, so the opportunities are far greater. What only the well-to-do enjoyed in an earlier clime is now considered a required basis for everyone. These 20th Century developments suggest new approaches as the 21st Century draws near. The idealism and simplicity of our young will doubtless lead to some very real efforts at forward progress.

Let us assume that perhaps 90% of the young wish to be constructive and do have a respect for acceptable living standards and responsible patterns of behavior, coupled with widespread compassion. It becomes their problem to keep their feet on the ground while new solutions are being found, and the young can keep their peers in line better than anyone else can. A diminution of the rioting suggests that they are already demonstrating some intelligent approaches.

Every generation should carry further than the previous one if civilization is to keep moving forward.

As my generation gradually yields the reins, it turns over the world in a far more advanced state than when it received them. The pleasures of a cultured society can be enjoyed by the many, and bodily well being is shared on a broader basis than ever before. We pass on the torch with pride and ask the dear young people to carry it ever higher. It is up to them.

* * *

This vacation is almost over. The return trip on the elegant *Paquebot France* was a delight—good conversation, excellent food, and the good sense on the part of the management to leave you alone when that is what you wanted.

New York came next. The most stimulating of cities, it combines numerous superlatives. Just name it; they have it; brilliance in business, stores on upper Fifth Avenue and its environs that offer you the quintessence of what the U.S. and the world provide. Where is there another Bergdorf-Goodman, Tiffany, Steuben with their incomparable creations? I was making business calls and some mornings walked down Park Avenue to my appointments. The Park Avenue skyline has a majesty all its own that grows on you. It has sheer stature combined with some extra space, for the planted areas in the center of the avenue and the numerous fountains provide a proportion that the Wall Street area does not have. It is breathtaking in its way.

And the brains in the New York business area match the size of the buildings. I had a couple of hours with Dr. Jim O'Leary at U.S. Trust. His gentle manner, excellent training and broad philosophical approach to business problems make him one of the country's most accurate business analysts. The mere fact that Jim O'Leary is on their staff attests to the business astuteness of U.S. Trust Co. Robert Johnson at Paine Webber is another one of my favorites. With the good sense to distinguish between the charlatans and the quality businessmen, he has demonstrated a very acute sense of catching the latest inflections in business psychology. The breadth of point of view of New York businessmen never fails to impress me. Being here this time during the Nixon-McGovern campaign has been very interesting. Enough strengths and weaknesses were pointed out in both teams that I gained the impression that there will be many problems whoever wins. This is a very different approach from the desk pounding of partisans.

I went out to the Metropolitan Museum one afternoon. This time their special displays included a history of musical instruments and many interesting and incongruous-looking pieces; there was a series of Iranian miniature paintings and another of French drawings. Theatre included (for me) *Jesus Christ Superstar* —a jumble if I ever saw one—a little bit of everything, but at least the young people in it were having a marvelous time putting it on. And then there was Robert Morse, the most gifted and understated of comedians .in a play that did not come up to him—*Sugar*.

One morning as I was walking past Steuben Glass there was a beautiful red Irish setter cavorting about in the sizable pond outside the building. He was having the most wonderful time, biting the water and actually smiling. When he was finished with his ablutions his young hippy master, who was sitting on the edge of the pool, patted his head, the dog hopped out, and the two walked off together—Tom Sawyer and his dog on Fifth Avenue.

The restaurants were superb, as is to be expected of New York's greats: this time Sardi's with its warmth and local color and good nature, the exquisite Tower Suite with elegant food and its incomparable view of both the East River and the Hudson River (including this evening the *Kungsholm* nestled far below at its pier). There was a night at Trader Vic's with gardenias floating in the cocktails and a dinner out under the stars on the most perfect of New York's evenings at Tavern on the Green. The beautiful skyline served as a boundary while young people of all races played on the adjoining green. It is a sad commentary on inflation that one hardly needs to make a reservation any more at New York's great restaurants, and many of the greatest, like Colony, Baroque and Chauveron's, have closed. People at every level are having to reduce their spending habits. And it is the luxury items that are the first to go. Colleges, symphonies, and art galleries may be among the next casualties.

Then there was Labor Day weekened in Connecticut, up in Warren, the most charming of tiny New England hamlets, with white painted houses and green shutters, gently rolling hills and beautiful wooded areas with ferns abounding. Wherever one looks there are trees and ferns, and there is a pond in the garden with frogs. This is the spot where my sister and her husband retreat when they need to escape the tensions of New York City. And there peace abides.

Came the trip home, always a treat, for America is spread in her vastness before the eyes of the train rider, mercifully protected by Amtrak, which deserves widespread public support. There is stylish Chicago, clean and windswept, a tribute to Mayor Daley's government. Then came the mighty Mississippi—watershed of the nation—the neat grain fields of Iowa and Nebraska, and an absolute myriad of stars. Lying in bed on the train I could look right up at the gorgeous display. There had been such cloudy skies on the Atlantic and in France that stars had been hardly visible this summer. And then one approached the awesome Rockies—there are few such mountains in the world. We wend our way through the spectacular canyons, the interesting rock formations of Wyoming, the lovely Wasatch Range in Utah, lonely stretches of Nevada and the brief glimpse of the gambling denizens of Reno, which boasts of being the "biggest little city in the world." Comes next the spectacular beauty of the high Sierras, a haven for those who love natural beauty. California is blessed with God-given scenery. Then we come down through the fruit orchards of the foothills and into the fertile central valley, breadbasket of California. And it's home again to stately, dignified old Sacramento, with its spreading elms, sparkling gold and white Capitol dome and the pretty apartment that is home to me.

A kind friend has met me, and there are my beautiful

paintings and sculpture all to be enjoyed again. I step out on the terrace and see Mt. Diablo in the far off distance and the Sacramento River threading its way through fertile farm lands.

It's a beautiful magnanimous country, the epitome of what the 20th Century has created. A thought keeps recurring to me. Sturdy people built this country. Intelligence and backbreaking hard work combined with imagination and lofty ideals all went in to the effort. But today we hear much talk of splinter groups and there is little emphasis on intelligence and ability. Selection by quota will not solve our problems. We need our finest minds as never before. And hopefully we can once more place being Americans before being members of various factions. In the rest of the world intense local loyalties brought more problems than peace. Hopefully we can retain the love of country which helped us build and put all the U.S.A. above its parts.

* * *

Other activities which might be mentioned here are membership on the Boards of the Mercy General Hospital Foundation (I am also an officer), the Sacramento Symphony Trust Foundation, and the Y.M.C.A. Trust Foundation. Hopefully my service with these excellent bodies can make some small contribution. The dedication, wit, and high intelligence of the Sisters of Mercy are an inspiration to all who work with them. I hope society fully appreciates them. The constructive manner in which the Ford Foundation provided funds for symphonies all over the country has given a real impetus to the maintenance of culture during a period when inflation is threatening its existence. It will take our best efforts to keep these institutions alive. It would be a tragedy if the ravages of inflation can destroy the 20th Century advances in the areas of humanity and gentle living. Vietnam and welfare excesses are too high a price to pay for that sacrifice.

EPILOGUE

"THE MOVING finger writes, and having writ moves on."*

And here it is, my narrative, once over lightly of a very happy hardworking life as it has paralleled the passing years of the 20th Century.

A verse on a sundial says, "I only count the hours that shine."

Perhaps, dear reader, you may think my life unusually benign. I had many blessings to count. And this is what I remember. But let it also be mentioned that there were acute personal problems to face in addition to the wars and Depression which are recited here. Recurring health problems have been a constant trial. Many bouts of bronchitis and several of pneumonia in my childhood left a latent tuberculosis hazard, fortunately controlled. Twenty years of a bleeding stomach ulcer led to the removal of five-sixths of my stomach. My life routine has never been the same since, and living with a crippled digestive apparatus is a major accommodation to master. These hazards are mentioned for one reason only. They made many of the activities heretofore described much harder of realization than would otherwise have been true, and should remind any young people who perchance may read these words and who sometimes become deeply discouraged that others have also had mountains to climb. Bad health can provide a major interference with one's personal life and did in this instance, but it can be met. Every life has its peaks and valleys. One's trials can become a test of one's metal.

However, I have been blessed with love and given and received of that wonderful attribute. Love brings a glow to one's life and activities, and a life without it would be a sorry one indeed. Love is like quicksilver in the palm of your hand.

*Quotation from the Rubaiyat of Omar Khayyam.

Clutch it too tightly and it may slip away. Let it rest gently, and it is yours forever.

We cannot foresee the future. No one knows what is around the bend.

We have been living through a particularly serious re-examination of our standards. We could succumb to another period like' the dark ages or the trauma of the French Revolution, but we do not have to. If we are truly the children of the civilized society which we believe we have created, we should be able to preserve a measure of progress by combining a broad sense of justice, a lively imagination, and superior intelligence with industry, self-discipline, common sense and love. We can keep our forward-looking society moving in the right direction. We probably need a little more confidence in our own sense of values so that the attacks of the fringe groups and troublemakers do not upset our equilibrium. We can remember what it means to be an American in the finest sense of that word. Let us never descend to the lowest common denominator, but keep inching up to our highest capacity. It's the only full way to live.

And so, my beloved country, I toast your future. Our 200th birthday is just around the corner. Let us make sure that the best is yet to come.

I salute my wonderful family. I say thank you for our beautiful young people. How could we have been so lucky?

For myself, I shall keep my eyes on the stars. Many goals still lie ahead. I think often of Bobby Kennedy's quotation at Atlantic City, "For I have promises to keep, and miles to go before I sleep."

"And where my loved ones wait, I come gently on."*

September, 1972

*Source unknown.